THE ULTIMATE ATTACHMENT THEORY WORKBOOK

Uplevel Your Emotional Intelligence, Deepen Relationships, Cultivate Healthy Family Bonds, and Build **Lasting Love** in Modern Times

HELEN HARPER

© 2026 by Bronnenmore LLC
Published under the pen name Helen Harper

All rights reserved.

No part of this book may be reproduced, distributed, transmitted, stored in a retrieval system, or translated into any form or by any means—electronic, mechanical, photocopying, recording, or otherwise—without the prior written permission of the publisher, except for brief quotations in reviews or scholarly works.

Worksheets may be photocopied for individual personal use only. Classroom, group, or commercial use requires prior written permission from the publisher.

This book is intended for educational and informational purposes only. It is not a substitute for professional psychological, medical, legal, or therapeutic advice, diagnosis, or treatment. The author is not a licensed therapist, psychologist, or medical professional, and the information contained herein should not be used as a replacement for consultation with qualified professionals. Readers are encouraged to seek appropriate professional guidance for their individual circumstances.

While the publisher has made every effort to ensure the accuracy and completeness of the information contained in this book, no representations or warranties are made with respect to the accuracy, applicability, fitness, or completeness of the contents. The publisher assumes no responsibility for errors, omissions, or outcomes resulting from the use of this material.

All trademarks referenced herein are the property of their respective owners and are used for identification purposes only.

Any references to individuals, relationships, or scenarios are either fictionalized or anonymized for illustrative purposes. Any resemblance to actual persons or events is purely coincidental.

Attachment theory concepts discussed in this book are derived from established psychological research and theory; however, interpretations and applications reflect the author's synthesis and perspective.

ISBN: 979-8-9943337-0-9 (eBook)
ISBN: 979-8-9943337-1-6 (Paperback, black & white interior)
ISBN: 979-8-9943337-2-3 (Hardcover, color interior)
ISBN: 979-8-9943337-3-0 (Audiobook)

This book is dedicated to Kristi K.–
The safe space you gave us transformed our attachment.
You bettered the partners we are and the people we are becoming.
This book is my attempt to pay your gift forward.

CONTENTS

	Introduction: The Conversation That Changed Everything	vii
01	Understanding Attachment Theory	1
02	Personal Growth and Emotional Intelligence	33
03	Cultivating Healthy Relationships	81
04	Enhancing Family Bonds	135
05	Addressing Trauma and Healing	179
06	Navigating Modern Relationship Challenges	211
07	Holistic Well-being and Relationship Building	259
08	Sustaining Growth and Transformation	287
	Conclusion: Returning to Yourself, Reaching for Connection	307
	Author's Note	309
	References	311

INTRODUCTION

The Conversation That Changed Everything

I buried my hands in the suds of my older brother's kitchen sink, scrubbing the bottle parts and teething toys as quietly as possible, my hands red and knuckles white. My six-month-old son finally fell asleep in the guest room: a space crowded with a blow-up mattress, a pack-and-play, loose diapers, and the bags of baby gear I threw together to leave home. The absence of my son's cries and coos amplified the storm of thoughts I tried to suppress.

My brother's familiar presence lingered only in a silent, cooled cup of half-drunk coffee he abandoned in his rush to work. I add that to the suds and scrub, pushing up the sleeves of my soft nursing top from Target, tucking a loose strand of unbrushed hair behind my ear.

I jolted at the soft knock on the door.

This was the conversation I couldn't stall anymore. I rehearsed my words. I tried to steel myself for every possible outcome. Would I be heard this time? Would my resolve hold? Would this be the moment everything changed?

I dried my hands on a lightly used burp cloth and went to the door, my bare feet barely audible. I turned the knob.

Paul stood outside, his sturdy arms and calloused hands hanging at his sides. He was dressed in familiar athletic shorts, a t-shirt, sandals, and his white gold wedding band. White gold, because the metal would be easy to remove should anything harm his hardworking hands. I chose something he could wear all the time, but in our seven years of marriage, it rarely made an appearance.

Still, he looked like the man I thought I knew, not the stranger I had been coexisting with for months. The warmth in his brown eyes and the softness in his expression hit me like a wave. I loved this man.

And yet, just seconds before, I had been sure—absolutely sure—our marriage was over.

I swallowed a breath of doubt as he stepped inside. How was this going to go? Would it be like every other time?

I often look back and wonder how different things might have been if I had discovered the world of attachment theory sooner.

Because attachment theory didn't just help me understand *why* things were breaking. It showed me *how* to rebuild—brick by emotional brick—with clarity, intention, and hope. It gave me language for needs I had long buried. It revealed the patterns beneath my panic. And slowly, it offered me a way forward—not just in my marriage, but in every relationship I carried.

This book was born from that journey.

Why This Book?

This is not another academic breakdown of attachment theory, nor is it a romantic how-to guide. This is a practical, trauma-informed workbook designed to help you make real and lasting changes in your self-understanding, relationships, and emotional blueprints.

Yes, you'll learn the basics. But more importantly, you'll learn how to apply them. Secure attachment isn't just something we seek; it's something we must practice.

Unlike many books that focus on a single type of relationship, this one reaches across the entire spectrum: romantic partnerships, family bonds, friendships, workplace dynamics, and, most importantly, your relationship with yourself.

This book is structured to guide you inward first, and outward second. We begin by helping you identify your attachment style and explore how it shows up in your life. Then, we move into real-world application—how these patterns play out in intimacy, parenting, friendships, and beyond. The latter half of the book dives deeper: trauma, generational influences, digital dynamics, holistic wellness, and how to sustain what you've built.

You will be learning *and* doing.

How to Use This Book

Throughout the chapters, you'll find tools designed not just to inform, but to transform. Here's what to look for:

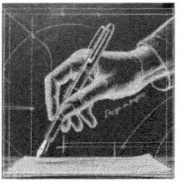

Individual Activities—Personal reflections, assessments, and journal prompts to deepen insight

Partner Activities—Exercises to explore attachment with those you love

Case Studies—Real-life stories to help concepts come alive

Tools—Visuals, checklists, and guides to help reinforce what you've learned

Guidance for Lasting Change—Practices and rituals to support long-term transformation

Who Is This Book For?

This book is for the person ready to stop cycling through confusion and start showing up with clarity. It's for anyone who wants to stop reacting out of fear and start relating from security. It's for the self-aware and the curious—the weary and the hopeful—the ones who are done repeating patterns that keep them lonely, disconnected, or unseen.

Whether you're a young adult navigating early relationships, a parent attempting to break cycles, or someone rebuilding after rupture—this book will meet you where you are. And then walk alongside you as you evolve.

One Last Note Before You Begin

You do not need to be perfect to be worthy of secure love. You do not need to have had a secure beginning to build a secure future.

What you *do* need is willingness.

The willingness to notice. To pause. To feel. To try again.

The willingness to be just 5% more honest, 5% more open, 5% more kind—to yourself and to the people you love.

This is your invitation to begin that work. To rebuild your emotional blueprint with steady hands and a brave heart.

There will be no test at the end of the book. However, there will be evidence in how you speak to yourself, interact with others, and trust yourself to love again.

You aren't starting from scratch. You're starting with experience. Now, let's turn it into wisdom.

01

Understanding Attachment Theory

"You wore your ring." I dipped my chin toward his hand.

"Can I come in?" he asked, voice calm.

I moved aside, following his movements with tight eyes. Paul took a seat at the edge of the family-room sectional, shoulders drawn forward, elbows on his knees, hands clasped together.

Normally, his body would be restless—attention split, energy darting around the room like he couldn't keep pace with everything pressing in. But now, for once, he was still. His attention was fixed on me—steady, subdued.

Something in me loosened. My pulse slowed. My chest let go of a tension I hadn't even realized I was holding.

Maybe—maybe—this conversation could happen.

"Is Alex sleeping?" he asked.

"He just went down maybe ten minutes ago." I took a seat next to him, back straight, and turned my knees toward him, holding both hands in my lap.

We exchanged polite updates on the previous week, settling into the space like people returning to a room they once called home. I felt the moment come together. My mouth was dry. My heart hammered against my ribcage. I swallowed hard. "Paul, I wanted to talk with you about us. About how things have been."

He stiffened, just slightly, as though bracing for impact. But he said nothing.

> "I know the last two years have been a challenging time for you. You've done a lot of healing—and based on what you've shared, and what I've seen, I believe you're healthier now."

My pulse quickened. My palms began to sweat.

> "But you don't seem interested in me anymore. You don't sit with me, or look at me, or ask how I'm doing. You don't touch me. You seem angry a lot of the time—and I feel like you blame me for it."

His breathing sped up and his eyes widened, but he said nothing. Usually, he would've cut me off by now. Deflect. Reframe. Shut the conversation down before I ever finished my thought. But this time, he didn't flinch. He didn't interrupt. That alone made the room feel unfamiliar—like something shifted or cracked open.

So, I kept going.

I gave examples—not to accuse, but to name.

The nights he came home and disappeared into his phone.

The weeks he hadn't asked me a single personal question.

The days I was sick while caring for our infant, he offered neither touch nor tenderness.

Still, he stayed quiet.

> "I want you to be happy, Paul. I just don't feel like you are. Not with me. And it feels like... You don't love me anymore."

I took a long breath.

> "And if that's true, then maybe we both deserve more. You deserve someone you love. I deserve to feel loved."

Another breath. This one was steadier.

> "Things need to change."

At the time, I lacked the words to express what was going on beneath the surface of our relationship. I only knew I was longing for connection, but coming up empty.

What I later discovered through attachment theory gave everything a name: the anxiety, the distance, and the spiral we couldn't seem to break free from.

We were both reacting to attachment patterns that predated our relationship. Patterns had nothing to do with love, but everything to do with safety. Everything changed once I understood those patterns, both mine and his.

In this chapter, we'll unpack what attachment theory is, how it forms, and how it shows up in our most important relationships. Before we can change the blueprint, we need to learn how to read it.

Origins of Attachment: A Historical Perspective

Attachment theory took shape in the 1950s with the groundbreaking work of British psychiatrist John Bowlby, who challenged the behaviourist view that affection and emotional bonds were secondary to basic needs like food and shelter. Bowlby argued that human beings are biologically wired to seek connection, especially in infancy, and that early relationships with primary caregivers form the blueprint for future emotional development.[1]

Building on Bowlby's foundation, developmental psychologist Mary Ainsworth introduced the *Strange Situation* study, a structured observation of how infants responded to separations and reunions with their caregivers. Her research identified consistent patterns of behavior that revealed differing levels of security in the attachment bond. These patterns—secure, anxious, and avoidant—became the basis for what we now recognize as attachment styles.[2]

As research progressed, attachment theory extended beyond childhood to explore how early relational experiences shape adult behaviors, particularly in romantic relationships, emotional regulation, and interpersonal trust.[3] What began as a theory of infant development gradually evolved into a comprehensive framework for understanding the emotional fabric of human connection across the lifespan.[4]

Today, attachment theory is deeply embedded in contemporary psychology and therapeutic practice. It offers a powerful lens for understanding not just how we relate to others, but also how we respond to stress, seek comfort, and build (or struggle to build) intimacy. Therapists use attachment-informed approaches to help individuals and couples identify recurring patterns, heal relational wounds, and develop healthier ways of connecting.[4]

Understanding the historical context helps us appreciate attachment theory's long-term relevance. It's more than just an academic concept; it's a practical, emotional tool that continues to influence how we perceive ourselves and our relationships.

With this foundation in place, we can now look at the four core attachment styles—secure, anxious, avoidant, and disorganized—and how they manifest in everyday relationships.

The Four Attachment Styles: Secure, Anxious, Avoidant, and Disorganized

Understanding attachment styles helps us decode the often-invisible patterns that shape how we give and receive love, reassurance, and emotional support. These styles—secure, anxious, avoidant, and disorganized—don't just show up in romantic relationships. They echo through our friendships, our families, and even how we parent or are parented.

Let's take a closer look:

1. Secure Attachment: "I'm okay, you're okay."

People with a secure attachment style are generally comfortable with closeness, but not dependent on it. They trust easily, communicate clearly, and can both give and receive emotional support without fear of losing themselves in the process.

ROMANTIC EXAMPLE:

Elena and Jordan are in a long-distance relationship. When Jordan doesn't respond to a message right away, Elena doesn't panic or assume the worst. She trusts Jordan's commitment and feels secure in their bond. When they reconnect, she might say, "Hey, missed you today," without judgment or fear of rejection.

FRIENDSHIP EXAMPLE:

David and Chris have been friends for years. When Chris forgets David's birthday, David feels hurt, but he doesn't question their entire friendship. Instead, he expresses his feelings directly: "That bummed me out—I was really hoping to hear from you."

PARENT-CHILD EXAMPLE:

A securely attached child falls down at the playground and runs to their caregiver. The caregiver soothes them warmly. The child feels safe, comforted, and then confidently returns to play—trusting the caregiver's presence and responsiveness.

2. Anxious Attachment: "I'm not okay unless you reassure me constantly."

Anxiously attached individuals often crave closeness but fear abandonment. Their internal narrative sounds like: *"If you don't respond, you must not care."* They may misinterpret neutral cues as rejection, driven by heightened cortisol responses and a constant search for reassurance.

ROMANTIC EXAMPLE:

Sam sends a vulnerable text to his partner and doesn't hear back for a few hours. His heart races. He rereads the message, second-guesses himself, and sends follow-ups like, *"Are you mad?"* or *"Did I do something wrong?"* The silence feels threatening, triggering panic rather than patience.

FRIENDSHIP EXAMPLE:

Marissa feels hurt when her best friend makes weekend plans without her. Instead of addressing it openly, she withdraws or posts vague, sad messages on social media, hoping her friend will notice and reassure her.

PARENT-CHILD EXAMPLE:

An anxiously attached child might cling to their caregiver even when it's safe to explore. Their play is frequently interrupted by checking in. They're not sure if the caregiver will stay attuned, so they stay close to avoid emotional danger.

3. Avoidant Attachment: "I'm okay, but you're a little too much."

Avoidantly attached individuals often value independence over intimacy. Closeness can feel suffocating, and vulnerability is quietly avoided. The dominant belief is that *relying on others isn't safe—* better to take care of yourself.

ROMANTIC EXAMPLE:

When asked, "What are you feeling?" Scott freezes. His partner wants emotional closeness, but Scott changes the subject or shuts down. Emotional intensity activates his internal alarm system. Deep down, he fears that needing others will lead to disappointment or loss of control.

FRIENDSHIP EXAMPLE:

Nina's friends describe her as reliable but hard to "get close to." She shows up for events but rarely shares personal details. When a friend vents about a distressing day, Nina changes the topic or gives practical advice instead of empathizing.

PARENT-CHILD EXAMPLE:

An avoidantly attached child may seem unusually independent—rarely asking for help, not showing distress when separated from their caregiver. But this self-reliance is often a learned adaptation to emotional unavailability.

4. Disorganized Attachment: "I want closeness, but I'm scared of it."

Disorganized attachment is the result of deeply conflicting messages: *"Come here—no, stay away."* It often stems from trauma, abuse, or caregivers who were both a source of comfort and fear. These individuals desperately want connection but don't trust it.

ROMANTIC EXAMPLE:

Talia alternates between clinging and pushing her partner away. One moment, she begs not to be left alone; the next, she picks a fight and storms out. The emotional unpredictability reflects her inner chaos: love is both a lifeline and a threat.

FRIENDSHIP EXAMPLE:

Liam forms fast, intense friendships, but soon becomes paranoid that his friend will betray or abandon him. He might lash out over imagined slights or abruptly ghost, overwhelmed by a sense of mistrust or shame.

PARENT-CHILD EXAMPLE:

A disorganized child may run to their caregiver for comfort, then hit or hide. The child's body wants safety—but their brain, shaped by early fear, doesn't know whether the caregiver will soothe or harm them. The result is confusion and emotional dysregulation.

Why This Matters

Attachment styles shape more than our relationships—they shape us. They influence how we seek comfort, handle conflict, and experience trust. Though rooted in early experiences, attachment is not fixed. Thanks to neuroplasticity, our brains can adapt. New relationships, therapy, and self-reflection can gradually revise the emotional blueprints we carry.[3]

Securely attached individuals tend to experience greater emotional resilience and well-being, while insecure styles—anxious, avoidant, or disorganized—are often linked to higher rates of anxiety, depression, and interpersonal difficulties.[5] But these patterns are not life sentences. They are adaptive responses that made sense once, and can be unlearned with intention and support.

By becoming aware of your own attachment style, you gain more than insight—you gain the power to choose differently. When you recognize a pattern, you can interrupt it. When you name your needs, you invite connection. When you understand your past, you create space for a different future.

So how do you begin identifying your attachment style?

Start by observing your responses to closeness, separation, and emotional vulnerability. Consider how you react when someone moves away or gets too close. Do you lean in, turn away, cling, or disconnect?

These questions are intended to reveal the patterns that silently guide your relationships rather than to label them. Once illuminated, they can be changed.

Now that we've looked at how attachment styles develop and why they're important, let's look at the science behind them: how our brains and nervous systems drive these patterns in the first place.

The Science Behind Attachment: Brain and Behavior

The Messengers

We can't understand attachment without discussing its chemistry. The bonds we form with others are heavily influenced by the brain's neurochemical cocktail, particularly oxytocin, dopamine, and cortisol. Consider this common relational scenario:

> Imagine a woman named Maya who just started dating someone new. In the beginning, every text message, every smile, every small gesture from her partner triggers a dopamine release. This neurotransmitter is tied to the brain's reward system, reinforcing behaviors that feel pleasurable and motivating Maya to seek more connection. This "honeymoon high" can feel addictive—dopamine is the same chemical pathway activated by gambling or chocolate.

As the relationship progresses and physical intimacy is introduced, oxytocin, also known as the "bonding hormone," comes into play. Oxytocin is released during physical contact, particularly during sex or extended eye contact. In Maya's brain, oxytocin promotes trust, closeness, and a sense of safety with her partner. It encourages her brain to associate this person with "home."

Fast forward for Maya and her partner; imagine she texts her partner and receives no response for hours. Cortisol, a stress hormone, increases over time. Her heart races, and her thoughts swirl: Did I say something *wrong*? Are they losing interest? This is where attachment patterns begin to emerge. If Maya has an anxious attachment style, her cortisol response may be heightened, increasing her likelihood of panic, overthinking, or seeking reassurance. In the absence of soothing input (such as a returned message), her brain perceives silence as a threat, and her nervous system responds accordingly.

Meanwhile, if her partner has an avoidant attachment style, *their* brain might be flooded by cortisol in the face of emotional closeness or conflict, prompting them to withdraw as a self-protective mechanism.

So you see, our attachment behaviors aren't just learned—they're wired, mediated by chemicals that either help us connect or signal threat. Understanding this helps us approach our relationships with greater compassion—not just for others, but for ourselves.

The Interpreters

Working in tandem with the chemistry of our attachment brain is the brain's architecture.

Let's return to Maya.

She's still in that new relationship—the texts have slowed, her chest feels tight, and her thoughts are spiraling. What's happening here is more than just emotional or chemical; it's also *neurological*.

At the heart of this inner storm is the amygdala—an almond-shaped cluster buried deep in the brain's limbic system. Its job? To scan for danger. Fast, reactive, and ancient, the amygdala doesn't waste time on nuance. It doesn't ask, *"Did Josh just get busy at work?"* It screams, *"Something's wrong. You're about to be left. ACT NOW."*

This hypervigilant system served our ancestors well when the threat was a rustle in the tall grass or a shift in a tribe member's tone. In modern relationships, however, it can become overactive, particularly in people with insecure attachment histories. The amygdala cannot distinguish between being ignored and being emotionally endangered. To Maya's nervous system, Josh's silence is like emotional starvation. Her body responds with cortisol, and her mind has catastrophic thoughts.

But there's another player in this story: the prefrontal cortex, specifically the medial and ventrolateral regions. This is the part of Maya's brain that slows down, reassesses, and says, "Let's think this through." It's where logic, empathy, and emotional regulation reside. Ideally, the prefrontal cortex and amygdala work in tandem: the alarm goes off, the thinking brain evaluates, and the system settles.

However, attachment wounds, particularly those formed early in life, have the potential to disrupt that partnership. In people with anxious or disorganized attachment styles, the prefrontal cortex may struggle to regulate the amygdala's alarm bells. Maya experiences a rush of emotion in the absence of reassurance, which feels urgent, overwhelming, and real, even if it is inaccurate.

Now imagine this: Maya takes a breath. She puts her phone down. She reminds herself, *"Josh has always shown up for me. This silence probably means nothing about my worth."* That single moment—where the prefrontal cortex steps in—is the foundation of healing. It's how the brain begins to rewire itself.

We can strengthen this regulatory pathway by engaging in therapy, practicing mindfulness, engaging in self-reflection, and maintaining safe and healthy relationships. We can teach the brain that not all silence indicates abandonment. Not all distance equals danger. The amygdala may still sound the alarm, but with time, the prefrontal cortex learns to whisper back, *"You're okay. You're* safe."

And that, in many ways, is the essence of secure attachment: feeling fear and having the inner capacity to move through it with grace.

GUIDED PRACTICE:
The 5-Minute Reset—Regulating Your Nervous System in Real Time

Purpose: To help calm the amygdala, re-engage the prefrontal cortex, and bring awareness to the body's attachment-driven responses when triggered by emotional discomfort (e.g., silence, conflict, perceived rejection).

Step 1: Notice Without Judgment (1 Minute)

Name it to tame it.

When something upsetting happens, say silently or out loud:

- "I feel activated."
- "This is an attachment flare-up."
- "My nervous system is doing what it learned to do."

Optional prompt:

"Right now, I notice my _____ (e.g., chest, stomach, throat) feels tight. I'm telling myself the story that _____ (e.g., they don't care, I did something wrong)."

Let the story be a *story*, not a fact.

Step 2: Anchor in the Body (1 Minute)

Get out of your head, into your body.

Try one or more of the following:

- Place one hand on your heart, the other on your belly.
- Breathe in for 4 counts, hold for 2, exhale slowly for 6.
- Gently press your feet into the floor and name 3 things you can see, 2 things you can hear, 1 thing you can feel.

Why this matters: This signals safety to your nervous system. You're grounding in the now, not the *what-if*.

Step 3: Re-engage the Thinking Brain (1 Minute)

Now that your body is calmer, help your prefrontal cortex step back online. Ask yourself:

- "What are three other explanations for what's happening right now?"
- "What would I say to a friend in this situation?"
- "What do I know to be true about this person's character or our connection?"

You're not gaslighting yourself—you're expanding perspective. You're shifting from threat mode to curiosity.

Step 4: Choose Your Next Move with Intention (1 Minute)

Now that you're more regulated, you can act—not react.

Options might include:

- *Wait 20 minutes* before texting or replying.
- *Journal* instead of sending.
- *Reach out* to a trusted friend for reflection—not validation.
- *Do nothing yet.* Trust that your urge to "fix" it right now may not be serving you.

Reminder: You're allowed to feel anxious without acting on anxiety.

Step 5: Affirm Your Inner Safety (1 Minute)

Close with self-connection. Repeat silently or out loud:

- "I am safe in this moment."
- "I am learning to trust myself."
- "My worth isn't based on someone else's behavior."
- "This is hard—and I am doing something different."

Feel into that: You're not abandoning yourself. This is how new attachment pathways form.

Practice Note: You won't always feel better immediately. But each time you do this, you are strengthening the connection between your body, brain, and sense of self. You are teaching your nervous system that it can feel big feelings—and survive them.

Other Implications

Recent advancements in science have shed even more light on these complex interactions. Neuroimaging studies have revealed how attachment experiences shape brain development, offering insights into why some individuals are more resilient than others. Longitudinal studies continue to uncover how attachment impacts life outcomes over decades, reinforcing its importance in our personal and relational growth.

Understanding these scientific foundations increases our appreciation for attachment theory's practical applications. Understanding attachment provides you with a universal translator that allows you to make meaningful connections despite differences. Recognizing these patterns empowers us to transform them, resulting in more fulfilling relationships.

In this intricate dance between brain and behavior lies the essence of human connection. As we delve deeper into this exploration of attachment science, remember that each insight offers an opportunity for growth and transformation. Whether navigating relational complexities or striving for personal development, the science behind attachment provides a foundation for understanding and enhancing our most cherished bonds.

Attachment in Non-Traditional Family Structures

Attachment theory was initially rooted in research on mother-infant pairs within traditional, nuclear families. But families today are far more diverse. Single parents, same-sex couples, blended families, foster and adoptive caregivers, communal households, and grandparents-as-primary-guardians all represent loving, functional family systems where secure attachment can—and does—flourish.[6]

The core ingredients of secure attachment remain the same, regardless of family structure: emotional attunement, responsiveness, and consistent caregiving. Children do not require a specific gender, number, or biological tie to their caregivers to develop emotional security.[1] What they need is to feel seen, safe, and soothed when distressed.[7]

Research increasingly supports this view. Studies of children raised in same-sex parent households, for example, show no differences in emotional health or attachment security compared to those raised in heterosexual households.[8] In adoptive families, the quality of post-adoption caregiving—not genetic ties—predicts attachment outcomes.[9] Even in households that face additional stressors, such as economic hardship or parental separation, protective factors like caregiver warmth and emotional availability can foster resilience and security.[10]

It's also important to recognize that children may form multiple attachment relationships. Bonds with grandparents, siblings, foster parents, or trusted teachers are not secondary; they can buffer children against adversity and enrich their emotional world.[11] Secure attachment is not a singular connection, but an ecosystem of safe relationships.

This perspective empowers carers in non-traditional families. It affirms that the quality of connection, not the family label, is most important. Attachment is about repeatedly demonstrating love, presence, and consistency.

The Intergenerational Transmission of Attachment

Attachment doesn't begin with us. Our patterns of connection are often shaped by the emotional environment in which we grew up—just as our caregivers were shaped by theirs. This ongoing cycle is known as the intergenerational transmission of attachment.[12]

Research shows that caregivers tend to unconsciously pass down their own attachment styles through subtle behaviors: how they respond to distress, whether they make space for emotional expression, and how they attune (or fail to attune) to their child's needs.[13] A parent who grew up feeling emotionally dismissed may struggle to validate their child's feelings, not out of malice, but because emotional attunement was never modeled for them.

One of the most important predictors of a secure attachment in children is not a caregiver's own attachment history, but whether they've made sense of it.[14] This process, known as earned security, involves reflecting on early experiences with honesty, compassion, and coherence.[15] Caregivers who have done this inner work are more likely to respond consistently and sensitively to their child, even if they themselves had insecure or traumatic upbringings.[16]

Neuroscience reinforces this concept. Repeated relational experiences shape the brain—what's been termed "experience-dependent development."[17] When caregivers become more self-aware and emotionally present, they can offer new relational patterns to their children, creating a more secure blueprint than the one they received.

Breaking the cycle is difficult, but possible. Secure attachment does not necessitate ideal parenting or partnering. Being present, curious, and willing to repair paves the way. Every act of reflection, every moment of repair, helps to disrupt inherited patterns and rewrite the emotional blueprint for future generations.

Secure attachment is, therefore, more than just a gift.

It is a legacy that we can decide to leave.

Cultural Influences on Attachment Styles

While attachment theory offers a powerful framework for understanding human connection, it's essential to recognize that it was originally developed within a Western cultural context. Ideas about closeness, independence, emotional expression, and caregiving vary significantly across cultures—and so do attachment behaviors.[18]

In Western societies, particularly in the United States and parts of Europe, emotional independence and self-expression are often encouraged from youth. This aligns with how secure attachment is typically defined in Western literature: the ability to explore independently while maintaining a sense of connection with caregivers.[2] However, in more collectivist cultures—such as Japan, Korea, or many Indigenous and Latin American communities—interdependence, group harmony, and deference to elders may be prioritized over individual autonomy.[19]

These cultural values influence what is considered a "healthy" or "secure" bond. For example, in Japan, a securely attached child may appear more dependent on their caregiver compared to Western expectations, yet this closeness is valued and adaptive within that cultural setting.[20] Similarly, some behaviors labeled "anxious" in one context may simply reflect norms of emotional expressiveness or familial closeness in another.[21]

Research also shows variation in the distribution of attachment styles across cultures. For instance, Ainsworth's original "Strange Situation" study found that German infants showed a higher prevalence of avoidant attachment behaviors.[22] However, later analysis suggested this may reflect cultural emphasis on early self-reliance rather than genuine emotional avoidance.[23]

These differences enrich our understanding of attachment theory. Cultural context helps us understand that attachment behaviors are shaped not only by individual experiences but also by the broader values, expectations, and parenting practices of the society in which a person is raised.

As our world becomes increasingly interconnected, it's important to apply attachment theory with cultural sensitivity. This means acknowledging that behaviors must be interpreted through both psychological and cultural lenses—and that secure attachment may look different across families, communities, and continents.

Ultimately, the core of secure attachment remains universal: the presence of trust, emotional safety, and attuned caregiving. How these are expressed, however, is profoundly shaped by culture.

Case Study: The Nakamura-Díaz Family—Cultural Awareness as Attachment Work

> *"Learning each other's culture was not just about food or holidays—it was about learning how to love each other in the language of safety."*

Background: Two Worlds, One Home

The Nakamura-Díaz family is a blended multicultural household living in the Bay Area.

- **Kenji (38, he/him):** Second-generation Japanese American, raised in a family where emotional restraint, respect for elders, and achievement were highly valued.
- **Camila (36, she/her):** Colombian immigrant, raised in a warm, expressive household where physical affection, direct communication, and extended family involvement were the norm.
- **Isabel (9, she/her):** Their daughter, born in the U.S., sensitive and observant, often caught between cultural cues that didn't always align.

Though deeply in love, Kenji and Camila sometimes struggled to reconcile their cultural emotional blueprints, especially when it came to parenting and emotional expression.

The Tension: When Emotional Worlds Collide

One evening, Isabel came home from school in tears after being excluded from a friend group. Camila immediately swept her into her arms, encouraging her to cry it out and talk through every detail.

Kenji, sitting nearby, quietly said,

> "We don't have to make this a big deal. She'll get through it."

Camila stiffened. Isabel pulled away.

Later that night, Camila confronted Kenji:

> "You shut her down. You do that with me too, sometimes."

Kenji, feeling misunderstood, replied:

> "In my family, we didn't talk about feelings all the time. We showed love by showing up, not by falling apart. I was trying to help her feel strong."

Both of them were trying to protect their daughter, but their instincts came from different cultural definitions of emotional safety.

The Shift: Choosing Cultural Curiosity Over Conflict

After a particularly tense week, the couple agreed to try something new: a family culture mapping exercise suggested by their therapist. Together, they created a chart comparing:

- How emotions were handled in each of their childhood homes
- What "support" looked like in moments of stress
- What messages they received (spoken or unspoken) about crying, comfort, and resilience

Camila shared how her parents *named* every feeling and stayed physically close. Kenji shared how his parents gave space out of respect, believing self-regulation was a form of love.

Both methods had value—but each came with blind spots.

- "We realized we weren't just parenting Isabel," Kenji said.
- "We were parenting our younger selves—and sometimes h protecting her from our past."

The Outcome: Co-Creating a Secure Family Culture

Kenji and Camila didn't try to erase their cultural instincts. Instead, they began consciously integrating both:

- When Isabel was upset, Kenji would ask:
- "Would you like some quiet or a hug—or both?"
- (Honoring both autonomy and comfort.)
- Camila began pausing before swooping in, giving Isabel a moment to lead the connection.
- As a family, they started a new tradition: "Heart Circle Sundays"—each person shared one high, one low, and one thing they needed that week.

Isabel flourished. She didn't have to pick a side—she learned that emotion could be expressed with both fire and calm, tears and stillness.

Narrative Insight: Why Culture Matters in Attachment

Attachment isn't only about how we bond—it's about how we understand what love looks and feels like. Culture shapes those expectations. When families become curious about each other's emotional roots, they create a new blueprint—one that holds more than one truth at a time.

> *"Secure attachment doesn't erase difference.*
> *It celebrates it—and makes space for all parts of the family to feel seen, safe, and valued."*

Generational Shifts in Attachment Perspectives

Beyond family systems and caregiving relationships, the cultural and historical moments in which we come of age shape attachment. Each generation absorbs values, norms, and relational expectations from the world around them. Economic shifts, social movements, and technological advances all leave their imprint—subtly molding how we express love, respond to intimacy, and form emotional bonds.[24]

Baby Boomers (born 1946–1964)

Raised in the wake of World War II, Baby Boomers were steeped in ideals of structure, duty, and stability. Traditional family roles and emotional restraint were often prized, particularly among men, contributing to attachment patterns marked by reliability but limited emotional expression. Bonds were frequently formed and maintained through shared responsibilities rather than overt emotional openness.[25]

Generation X (born 1965–1980)

Growing up during economic downturns, rising divorce rates, and increased dual-income or single-parent households, Gen X learned self-reliance early. Independence became both a necessity and a virtue. As a result, many developed avoidant attachment tendencies—viewing vulnerability as a liability and emotional dependence as risky.[26] Their relationships often prioritize equality and autonomy, sometimes at the expense of emotional closeness.

Millennials (born 1981–1996)

Millennials were encouraged to explore identity, values, and emotional health, coming of age amid the digital revolution and a cultural pendulum swing toward emotional openness. They seek relationships grounded in mutual growth, open communication, and authenticity. However, this emotional idealism can sometimes clash with real-world complexities—leading to anxious attachment tendencies when connection doesn't mirror their expectations.[27]

Generation Z (born 1997–2012)

Gen Z was born into a world already saturated with digital connections, social media, and cultural fluidity. They are emotionally literate and mental health-aware, but also deeply affected by constant online exposure, curated identities, and ambiguous relational norms like ghosting. This environment fosters a paradox: they long for meaningful connection yet often fear the vulnerability it requires. As a result, many swing between anxious and avoidant attachment patterns—seeking depth while navigating the superficiality of digital life.[28]

Generational Gaps and Emotional Misunderstandings

Each generation's unique relational blueprint can make cross-generational understanding a challenge. What one generation sees as emotional transparency, another may perceive as oversharing. Independence might be mistaken for coldness, while vulnerability might be misread as weakness.

These misunderstandings are often the result of differing survival strategies, each shaped by the emotional climate of the time. Stability and commitment are top priorities for Baby Boomers. Generation Xers frequently place a high value on space and autonomy. Millennials frequently focus on emotional processing, whereas Generation Z seeks meaning amid emotional noise.

Bridging the Divide

Bridging generational differences requires empathy and curiosity. Begin by listening without the intent to fix, judge, or debate. Invite stories rather than assumptions. Ask: *What shaped you? What mattered most during your formative years?*

Sharing experiences can help to bridge gaps. Organizing a family memory project, cooking a multigenerational meal, or discussing values across generations can promote unity while respecting differences. Most importantly, consider what unites us: the universal desire for safety, love, and understanding.

When we examine generational shifts through the lens of attachment, we can move beyond stereotypes. We begin to see the emotional survival strategies that lie beneath each generation's patterns, and as a result, we gain compassion not only for others but also for ourselves.

Identifying Your Attachment Style: A Self-Assessment Tool

By now, you've explored how attachment styles develop, how they are shaped by culture and generation, and how they influence your patterns of connection. But knowledge alone isn't the destination—it's the doorway. To begin shifting patterns, you first need to recognize them in yourself.

This subchapter invites you to do just that.

While identifying your attachment style can provide you with a handy label for clarity, it is not a fixed identity. We use these terms to describe how you've learned to feel safe, seen, and connected. When you uncover those patterns with compassion rather than criticism, you make room for healing and choice.

The following self-assessment tool is designed to help you begin this process. It draws from clinical research and therapeutic frameworks used to identify patterns of secure, anxious, avoidant, and disorganized attachment.[29] Through a series of questions and reflective prompts, you'll start to see how you typically respond to intimacy, conflict, and vulnerability in your closest relationships.

As you complete this assessment, keep in mind:

- **No style is "wrong."** Each one makes sense in the context of your emotional history.
- **Styles can shift.** With insight, support, and practice, people often move toward more secure attachment over time.[3]
- **You may relate to more than one style.** That's normal. Life experiences, relationship roles, and personal growth can shape how you attach in different contexts.

Think of this as a mirror instead of a verdict. You're not here to judge your reflection, but to understand it more fully.

This is the work of emotional awareness: noticing without rushing to fix or defend. By doing so, you begin the process of reconnecting with your true self and developing relationships based on trust, empathy, and mutual care.

When you're ready, go to the next page to start your self-assessment.

Attachment Style Self-Assessment Tool

Below is a clinically grounded self-assessment tool based on widely used frameworks, particularly the Experiences in Close Relationships (ECR) model and the Bartholomew & Horowitz four-category model of adult attachment.[29]

This tool is designed to help you better understand your attachment style. There are no right or wrong answers—only patterns that offer insight into how you relate to closeness, conflict, vulnerability, and connection.

Instructions:

- Read each statement carefully.
- Rate how true each statement feels for you on a scale of 1 to 5:
    - » 1 = Not at all true
    - » 2 = Slightly true
    - » 3 = Somewhat true
    - » 4 = Mostly true
    - » 5 = Very true

Use your initial, instinctive responses as they're often the most accurate reflection.

Part I: How I Experience Close Relationships

Statement	Rating (1–5)
I find it easy to get emotionally close to others.	
I am comfortable depending on others and having them depend on me.	

I worry that others won't value me as much as I value them	
I often fear that romantic partners will leave me.	
I prefer not to rely too heavily on others.	
I feel uncomfortable when people get too close to me.	
I want to be emotionally close, but I worry I'll get hurt.	
Sometimes I push people away even when I want connection.	
I often feel confused about how I feel in relationships.	
I find myself craving reassurance, even when I know I'm safe.	
I downplay my needs in relationships to avoid seeming "needy" or "too much."	
I struggle to trust that others will really be there for me.	
I get overwhelmed when people need too much from me emotionally.	
I want intimacy but fear people will let me down or reject me.	
When I'm upset, I either shut down or lash out, and then feel guilty or confused later.	

Part II: How I React During Conflict or Stress

Statement	Rating (1–5)
I seek comfort from someone close to me when I feel overwhelmed.	

I feel panic or distress when I think someone I love is pulling away.	
I distance myself when things get emotionally intense.	
I sometimes feel I don't deserve to be loved or supported.	
I have trouble calming down after emotional arguments.	

Scoring Guide (For Reflection Purposes Only)

There's no "score" to define you, but noticing your patterns can reveal which attachment tendencies may be most prominent.

Secure Attachment

Tend to score 4–5 on:

- "I find it easy to get emotionally close to others."
- "I am comfortable depending on others and having them depend on me."
- "I seek comfort from someone close to me when I feel overwhelmed."

You likely value intimacy and feel safe giving and receiving emotional support.

Anxious Attachment

Tend to score 4–5 on:

- "I worry that others won't value me as much as I value them."
- "I fear romantic partners will leave me."
- "I crave reassurance, even when I know I'm safe."

Your relationships may feel intense and vulnerable, with a fear of abandonment or being "too much."

Avoidant Attachment

Tend to score 4–5 on:

- "I prefer not to rely too heavily on others."
- "I feel uncomfortable when people get too close to me."
- "I downplay my needs to avoid seeming needy."

You may prize independence and emotional control but struggle to trust closeness.

Disorganized Attachment

Tend to score 4–5 on:

- "I push people away even when I want connection."
- "I get overwhelmed and either shut down or lash out."
- "I want intimacy but fear I'll get hurt or rejected."

You may feel conflicted—drawn to closeness, but afraid of it. Early relationships may have been inconsistent, neglectful, or even frightening.

Reflection Prompts:

1. Which items felt most true for you?
2. How have these patterns shown up in past or current relationships?
3. Which patterns do you want to better understand or begin shifting?
4. Who modeled emotional connection for you growing up—and what did that teach you about closeness or safety?

Final Note

This self-assessment is a starting point, not a diagnosis. If you recognize insecure patterns, know that change is possible. As you move through the rest of this book, you'll find tools to help you strengthen secure behaviors, deepen emotional insight, and build relationships rooted in safety and mutual care.

02

Personal Growth and Emotional Intelligence

"I don't understand," Paul finally said.

The confidence I had drawn from his earlier willingness to listen began to waver. Something inside me started to shrink.

"What's unclear?" I asked, careful not to sound defensive.

"You're my wife. I only want you as my wife. You do make me happy. I do love you. I'm trying to keep us afloat and keep us safe. I'm sorry if I've hurt you. I never meant to. You and our son... you're what matters most to me."

His voice cracked slightly. His brow furrowed. The edges of his mouth slackened. He looked like a man trying to grasp something just beyond reach—a man who meant every word and still didn't understand why they weren't enough.

I felt my chest tighten.

This was the part where I would usually rescue him. Soften. Offer comfort. Give him what I knew he needed to feel safe and validated. That's what I'd always done—manage the emotional temperature of the room, even if it burned me.

I opened my mouth to do it again.

But in a rare and quietly radical act of self-awareness, I closed it.

I sat in discomfort. I reminded myself that this moment mattered. If I softened now—if I prioritized peace over honesty—nothing would change. Despite his kind words and best intentions, the truth remained: I was drowning in a marriage that looked fine from the outside but felt hollow from the inside.

I took a breath. The panic in me—deeply wired, survival-shaped—begged me to let this go. To pretend it was just a misunderstanding. To believe this was close enough to love.

But I'd worked too hard to stop there.

> "I know you don't mean to hurt me, Paul. I believe that. But… I think there's a chance you don't even realize how unhappy you are. You're comfortable with me—and I get it, change is scary—but—"

> "I am happy with you. Don't tell me how I feel. They're my feelings."

His voice was calm but firm. My face flushed. He wasn't wrong.

> "Okay. That's fair," I said, catching myself, grounding again.

Another breath. Another reminder: You're not here to win. You're here to be honest.

> "I'm unhappy. I don't feel loved. I need things to change," I said.

He looked at me carefully.

> "What do you mean by change?"

I panicked again—my words spilling into solutions before my heart could catch up.

> "Well... like maybe we try some time apart for a while to regroup. Just a few weeks. I could stay with my mom, and you could—"
>
> "Wait. Helen." He interrupted gently, but clearly. "What does the worst-case scenario of 'change' look like to you?"

I froze. My throat tightened. This was the heart of it.

And I was terrified.

Not just of saying the words. But of what they might make real. I had spent so much of my life walking the emotional tightrope—reading rooms, avoiding conflict, trying to stay small enough to keep the peace. But this was the moment I had to decide: Was I willing to be misunderstood if it meant being truthful?

I could feel all my old patterns rising—urging to rescue, perform, self-abandon. But I also felt something new. The quiet, trembling voice of the woman I was becoming.

She had something to say. And this time, I was going to let her speak.

> "Worst-case scenario looks like separation. Divorce. Coparenting."

The responding silence was deafening.

In that moment—standing at the edge of truth with my heart in my throat—I realized that emotional growth doesn't always look graceful. Sometimes it looks like silence when you'd rather soothe. Like honesty when you're scared to lose someone. Like holding a boundary even when your whole body is screaming to retreat.

I had spent the majority of my life believing that love could only be earned by being good, agreeable, emotionally available, and easy to digest. And I married someone who had spent the majority of his life believing that safety came from control, structure, and keeping difficult emotions hidden.

Neither of us was trying to fail the other. However, both of us had attachment wounds that influenced how we gave and received love—and neither of us had the emotional tools to identify, regulate, or respond to what was going on beneath the surface.

We had to retrain ourselves. It wasn't the dramatic, tear-filled kind of work you see in movies—but the slow, often uncomfortable process of learning how to feel, pause, reframe, and respond. I began practicing mindfulness when I wanted to shut down. I learned to self-soothe instead of people-pleasing. I started looking inward to understand myself instead of blame, and to meet that understanding with compassion instead of shame.

This is what you'll learn in the chapters ahead.

You'll discover what emotional intelligence looks like in practice. You'll build your emotional regulation, self-awareness, mindfulness, and resilience. You'll reconnect with your inner child—the part of you that still craves love and safety—and learn how to parent them with presence and care.

Because the truth is that we can't have secure relationships with others if we keep abandoning ourselves.

And the journey toward secure attachment always begins here:

With presence.
With courage.
With one breath, one pause, one honest word at a time.

Emotional Intelligence:
The Key to Understanding Yourself

"Emotional intelligence is the act of intentionally embracing the power of emotions instead of being overpowered by them."

Imagine you're at a dinner party, balancing a plate of hors d'oeuvres and a glass of wine, when someone makes a comment that catches you off guard. Your heart races, your face warms, and your mind begins to spiral: *"Why did they say that?"* This is the moment emotional intelligence steps in to help you meet discomfort with awareness, regulation, and grace.

Emotional intelligence (EI) is the capacity to recognize, understand, and manage your own emotions—and to navigate the emotions of others with empathy and skill. Rather than being unaffected, you'll be attuned. Think of it as an internal compass, guiding you through the nuanced terrain of human emotion.[31]

Self-awareness is the foundation of EI. It allows you to notice what you're feeling and why. When a familiar frustration rises or anxiety creeps in, self-awareness helps you name it before it names you. This awareness is essential for making intentional rather than reactive choices.[32]

Self-regulation is the pause between impulse and action. Instead of snapping when irritated, you take a breath. Instead of shutting down, you stay present. Self-regulation means engaging emotion in a way that reflects your values rather than your stress.

Motivation is the fire in your belly that drives you to achieve your goals, leveraging emotions as fuel for persistence. Think of it as the engine that propels you forward even when the road gets bumpy.

This intrinsic drive helps you stay focused and committed, transforming challenges into opportunities for growth.

In relationships, emotional intelligence serves as a social lubricant, smoothing interactions and preventing friction. Improved communication is one of its most valuable gifts, allowing you to express yourself clearly and understand others without misinterpretation. It's similar to being fluent in the language of emotions, in which empathy serves as your translator. In conflict resolution, empathy allows you to put yourself in the shoes of another person, fostering understanding and defusing tension before it escalates.

Like any skill, emotional intelligence can be developed. The key is practice.

Emotional Intelligence Exercises

- **Journaling** your emotional experiences builds self-awareness. Over time, you'll start to notice patterns, triggers, and moments of growth.
- **Active listening** strengthens empathy. Practice being fully present when others speak—without planning your response. Listen to understand, not to reply.
- **Emotion identification** exercises refine your vocabulary. Are you overwhelmed or simply overstimulated? Disappointed or disheartened? The more precisely you can name your emotions, the more effectively you can manage them.
- **Perspective-taking** *builds empathy. Imagine how someone else might feel* in a given situation—not just what they did, but why they might have done it.

Whether you're navigating a difficult decision, working through conflict, or deepening a friendship, emotional intelligence is a tool you'll return to again and again.

Case Study: Alina—Learning to Listen Without Defending

Background:

Alina (she/her) is 28 years old, a second-generation American born to Eastern European immigrants. Raised in a household where emotional expression was often discouraged or interpreted as weakness, she learned early on to be self-contained, achievement-driven, and conflict-avoidant. Now, in her late twenties, she finds herself deeply in love with Tariq (he/him), a thoughtful and expressive man from a North African background where emotional attunement, extended family connection, and verbal processing are deeply valued.

At first, their differences fascinated her. Where she was measured, he was passionate. Where she leaned toward logic, he brought heart. But as the honeymoon stage faded, their cultural differences began to clash with unspoken attachment wounds.

The Conflict:

Tariq often shared his feelings openly: when he felt distant, when he felt dismissed, when he felt unheard. Alina, unfamiliar with such raw vulnerability, would freeze. She didn't know how to respond, so she defaulted to defensiveness or silence. Her internal narrative was: *"If I respond wrong, I'll be blamed. I'd rather say nothing than say the wrong thing."*

Tariq, in turn, interpreted her silence as emotional disinterest. This created a feedback loop of misinterpretation: he pursued closeness; she retreated. He raised concerns; she shut down. The very thing they both wanted—*a secure connection*—began to feel out of reach.

The Turning Point:
During one particularly emotional conversation, Tariq said quietly, *"I'm not asking you to fix how I feel. I'm asking you to feel it with me."*

That line echoed in Alina's mind for days.

She realized she wasn't lacking love but struggling with emotional fluency. She didn't have the tools to sit with discomfort, hers or his. So she began what she later called her "emotional unlearning" journey.

The Practice:
Alina committed to three small but powerful self-awareness and mindfulness exercises each week:

1. Mindful Pause Practice (Daily, 5 Minutes)
Each morning, Alina sat quietly and asked herself:
- *What am I feeling right now—emotionally and physically?*
- *Can I sit with that without needing to fix or justify it?*

This simple check-in helped her begin to name and normalize her emotions—sadness, guilt, nervousness—not just the easy ones like "busy" or "fine."

2. Emotion→Story→Truth Journaling (2x/Week)
When a difficult interaction occurred, she broke it down:
- **Emotion:** "I felt hurt when Tariq said I don't open up."
- **Story:** "My brain said, 'He thinks I'm cold and unlovable.'"
- **Truth:** "He's asking for connection, not criticizing me. I'm scared to be vulnerable."

This exercise slowed her automatic defense mechanisms and allowed space for reframe and repair.

3. Cultural Curiosity Conversations (1x/Week)
Once a week, Alina initiated intentional conversation with Tariq, asking questions like:
- *"What did love look like in your family growing up?"*
- *"What does emotional safety mean to you?"*

This shifted their dynamic from conflict to collaboration, creating a shared emotional vocabulary.

The Growth:

Over time, Alina became more comfortable naming her needs without guilt. When she felt overwhelmed, she began saying, *"I want to show up for you, but I need a moment to regulate first."* Tariq responded with patience and appreciation.

They both began to recognize emotional intelligence as a skill that deepens with practice, rather than a fixed trait. And in cross-cultural relationships, this skill is even more vital. Because beneath the different expressions of love, both partners are asking the same question: *"Can I be fully seen by you and still be safe?"*

Alina didn't become fluent overnight. But she became braver. And in doing so, her relationship became not just a mirror of her past, but a canvas for her becoming.

At work, EI enhances collaboration, leadership, and stress management. In families, it promotes trust and emotional safety. In romantic relationships, it shifts communication from defensive to connected.

Finally, emotional intelligence helps you understand yourself. It boosts personal development and improves social interaction. When you learn to identify, hold, and express your emotions with clarity and compassion, you will develop stronger relationships, more precise boundaries, and a more grounded sense of self.

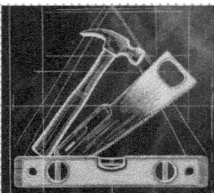

Emotional Vocabulary List

Cultivate a deeper language for your inner world. Emotions are not meant to be controlled or 'fixed,' but need to be felt and heard. Without this step, we often unintentionally surrender our driver's seat to them. The more precisely you can name your feelings, the more powerfully you can respond to them.

Joy & Interest	Sadness & Loss	Anger & Defensiveness	Fear & Anxiety	Shame & Guilt	Apathy & Confusion	Peace & Regulation	Disgust & Aversion
Admiring	Abandoned	Agitated	Alarmed	Ashamed	Aloof	Accepting	Appalled
Affectionate	Ashamed	Annoyed	Anxious	Cringey	Ambivalent	Aligned	Contemptuous
Amused	Defeated	Bitter	Apprehensive	Defeated	Attuned	At ease	Creeped out
Caring	Depressed	Contemptuous	Distrustful	Disgraced	Baffled	Balanced	Disapproving
Cheerful	Despairing	Defensive	Dreadful	Dishonored	Blah	Calm	Disdainful
Compassionate	Disappointed	Disgusted	Frightened	Embarrassed	Bored	Centered	Disenchanted
Confident	Fragile	Enraged	Helpless	Exposed	Checked out	Clear	Dismissive
Connected	Gloomy	Fed up	Hesitant	Flawed	Clingy	Content	Displeased
Content	Grief-stricken	Frustrated	Insecure	Guilty	Conflicted	Free	Grossed out
Curious	Grieving	Furious	Nervous	Humiliated	Detached	Grounded	Judgmental
Delighted	Guilt-ridden	Hostile	On edge	Impostor-ish	Disconnected	Harmonious	Loathing
Devoted	Heartbroken	Indignant	Overwhelmed	Inadequate	Disengaged	Mindful	Morally disturbed
Elated	Hopeless	Irritated	Panicked	Inferior	Dismissive	Present	Nauseated
Empowered	Hurt	Jealous	Paranoid	Mortified	Disorganized	Quiet	Repelled
Energized	Isolated	Mad	Shaky	Pathetic	Disoriented	Reassured	Revolted
Engaged	Let down	Outraged	Startled	Regretful	Distracted	Relaxed	Skeptical
Enthusiastic	Lonely	Pissed	Tense	Rejected	Empty	Restful	
Excited	Melancholy	Provoked	Terrified	Remorseful	Engulfed	Safe	
Fulfilled	Mournful	Resentful	Threatened	Self-conscious	Exhausted	Secure	
Giddy	Regretful	Seething	Timid	Unlovable	Flat	Serene	
Grateful	Vulnerable	Vengeful	Uneasy	Worthless	Foggy	Settled	
Hopeful	Weepy		Worried		Indifferent	Stable	
Inspired	Wistful				Misattuned	Still	
Intimate					Needy	Whole	
Joyful					Numb		
Nurturing					Preoccupied		
Playful					Puzzled		
Protective					Rejected		
Proud					Secure		
Radiant					Stagnant		
Safe					Stuck		
Satisfied					Torn		
Tender					Uninterested		
Trusting					Unmotivated		
Warm					Unsettled		
					Withdrawn		
					Yearning		

Mindfulness Practices for Emotional Regulation

Mindfulness is not a mystical practice reserved for mountaintop retreats. It's the simple, accessible act of paying attention to the present moment without judgment.[33] Like pressing "pause" on the remote control of a hectic day, mindfulness helps you return to yourself, recalibrate your nervous system, and regain emotional clarity.

When practiced regularly, mindfulness can enhance emotional regulation by strengthening your ability to stay grounded in the face of stress.[34] It heightens focus, reduces reactivity, and expands your capacity to respond with intention rather than impulse. Whether you're walking the dog, sipping tea, or navigating a tough conversation, mindfulness invites you to fully inhabit each moment.

Ever found yourself rereading the same sentence in a book without retaining a word? Or reacting sharply to a loved one without realizing why? These lapses in attention and control are common—but mindfulness trains you to notice what's happening inside you, as it happens.

 **Foundational Mindfulness Practices**

Mindful Breathing: Your breath is your anchor. To begin, sit or lie in a quiet space. Close your eyes. Inhale deeply, noticing the expansion in your chest. Exhale slowly. As thoughts arise, gently return your focus to your breath. Just five minutes a day can begin to rewire your stress response.[35]

Body Scan Meditation: This practice cultivates awareness of physical tension and invites relaxation. Lie down and close your eyes. Starting at your toes, slowly move your attention upward—feet, legs, hips, torso, shoulders, face—pausing to observe sensations in each area. There's no goal except awareness. This is especially helpful before sleep or during emotionally heavy days.

Mindful Eating: The next time you sit down to eat, remove distractions. Tune into the colors, textures, and flavors of your food. Chew slowly. Notice how the act of nourishing yourself feels. This practice builds gratitude and brings your attention out of your head and back into your body.

Morning Ritual: Begin your day with intention. Spend the first five minutes in stillness—either through mindful breathing or quiet reflection. This sets a calm foundation before the noise of the day begins.

The greatest gift of mindfulness is the space it creates between stimulus and response.[36] In moments of stress or overwhelm, mindfulness allows you to pause, assess, and choose your next move—rather than reacting from habit or emotional hijack.

Without mindfulness, stress might trigger irritation or withdrawal. But with practice, you learn to observe your inner state, ground yourself, and respond with clarity and calm. This emotional agility fosters resilience, reduces conflict, and strengthens relationships.

Case Study: "It's Just the Dishes" (The Emotional Hijack)

The Couple:
- David (he/him): 47, Gen X, career-focused, emotionally reserved, values structure and responsibility.
- Rachel (she/her): 34, Millennial, former marketing executive, currently a full-time mother to two young kids. Warm, expressive, exhausted.

Scene 1: The Argument (Without Tools)

It started over the dishes.

David walked into the kitchen after a long day at work and saw the sink full—again. Bottles, sippy cups, cereal bowls. He sighed audibly.

"I don't get it," he muttered. "You're home all day. How are the dishes never done?"

Rachel froze, her back still to him. The baby had been crying most of the afternoon. She hadn't eaten lunch. She hadn't even peed alone. And now, this.

"Wow," she snapped, turning around. "You think because I'm home I'm just lounging around? Must be nice to live in your world."

David's jaw tightened.

"I didn't say that. I'm just saying—it'd be great to come home and not feel like I have to pick up more work after working all day."

Rachel's voice rose:

"You think I'm not working?! I'm on-call 24/7! When's the last time you even bathed the kids without me walking you through it like a tutorial?"

David folded his arms.

"I don't even know how to talk to you anymore without getting yelled at."

Rachel scoffed.

"That's because you don't talk to me at all—unless it's to point out what I'm not doing."

Silence. Thick, hot, punishing silence.

Beneath the dishes and resentment were two broken truths:

Rachel felt unseen, overwhelmed, and starved for connection.

David felt dismissed, unappreciated, and lonely in a house full of people.

But instead of reaching for each other, they each retreated into old patterns—Rachel into fury, David into shut-down.

They went to bed in opposite corners, both carrying the ache of being misunderstood.

Scene 2: The Same Moment, With Emotional Intelligence

David walked into the kitchen, exhausted. The sink was full. He sighed, reflexively—but this time, he paused.

Rachel, sensing tension, turned to face him before he could speak. "I know the dishes are a mess. I didn't get to them."

David hesitated. He could feel the irritation bubbling. But he remembered what they'd been working on: assume good intent. Use feeling words. Stay curious.

"I noticed the mess, yeah. And honestly, my first feeling was frustration. But then I thought… maybe there's more going on."

Rachel blinked. Something in her body softened.

"There is. Today was… hard. The baby didn't nap. I didn't sit down. And I'm just so tired of feeling like I don't matter beyond being the default parent."

David exhaled. He stepped closer.

"That's not how I want you to feel. I think I've been assuming that because you're with the kids, you must be emotionally fulfilled. But maybe you're actually… depleted."

Tears welled in Rachel's eyes.

"I miss being your partner. I miss talking to you like a person, not just managing logistics. And I hate that we only seem to connect when something's wrong."

David reached for her hand.

"I miss you too. And I want to do better at showing up for us. Not just the house, or the kids. Us."

Rachel squeezed his hand. They didn't solve everything. The dishes were still in the sink. But now, there was warmth between them again. An ember of empathy, fanned by presence

Narrative Insight: The Difference Is the Doorway

In both versions, the pain was the same. The triggers were real. But the second version shows what happens when partners choose regulation over reaction, vulnerability over defense, and empathy over assumption.

Conflict isn't the enemy of intimacy—disconnection is.

When couples reach for tools instead of shields, they don't just solve problems: they *transform them*.

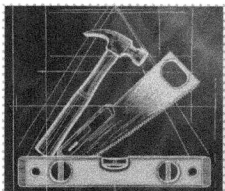
Mindful Practice Checklist

Use this guide to begin integrating mindfulness into your daily routine:

- ☐ **Mindful Breathing:** 5 minutes per day
- ☐ **Body Scan Meditation:** 10 minutes weekly
- ☐ **Mindful Eating:** 1 distraction-free meal per day
- ☐ **Morning Ritual:** 5 minutes of presence at the start of your day

Mindfulness does not have to be about silencing the mind or achieving serenity. It can be as simple as showing up for yourself, exactly as you are. Through consistent practice, you'll cultivate an inner refuge of calm. Not perfect, not polished, but present. And in that presence, you'll find power.

Self-Reflection: Exploring Your Emotional Landscape

If emotional intelligence is the compass, then self-reflection is the map. It assists you in navigating your inner world by identifying emotional patterns, understanding their origins, and making sense of your experiences. Without self-reflection, emotions can feel like sudden weather: unpredictable, overwhelming, and difficult to understand. However, with reflection, even the most intense emotional storm can be used to gain insight and grow.

Self-reflection is the practice of pausing to examine one's thoughts, emotions, and behaviors. Avoid over-analysis and self-criticism. Simply slow down long enough to ask yourself, "What is going on inside of me right now?"

Why Self-Reflection Matters

Many of us move through life on emotional autopilot, reacting to people and situations without fully understanding why. Self-reflection interrupts that cycle. It allows you to step back from reactivity and uncover the deeper layers beneath your emotional responses—old wounds, unmet needs, unspoken fears, or habitual beliefs.[37]

With regular practice, self-reflection enhances self-awareness, improves emotional regulation, and supports healthier relationships. It helps you:

- Recognize your emotional triggers
- Understand the patterns in your thinking
- Identify when you're projecting old experiences onto new situations
- Make intentional, values-aligned choices rather than reactive ones

Case Study: Trust Without Proof—Rossilyn and Cole

Background:

Rossilyn (29, she/her) ended a long-term relationship two years ago after discovering her partner had been unfaithful for over six months. The betrayal blindsided her; there had been no obvious signs, and her ex had frequently reassured her of his loyalty. Since then, Rossilyn has worked on rebuilding her life—new apartment, stable career, close friendships—but she's struggled to feel emotionally safe in dating.

Now, she's six months into a relationship with Cole (31, he/him), a kind and emotionally available man. Cole communicates clearly, follows through on plans, and expresses affection freely. Yet despite his consistency, Rossilyn finds herself guarded. She notices every time he glances at his phone, she hesitates to believe his reassurances, and she feels anxiety when she doesn't hear from him for a few hours.

Cole, though patient, begins to feel the impact. "It's like no matter what I do, I'm being measured against someone else's mistake," he says during a conversation. "I want to be here with you—but I also want to feel trusted."

The Pattern

Rossilyn recognizes that her fear isn't about Cole's behavior, but rather what her nervous system learned from past betrayals. She journals, "Even when I tell myself there's no red flag, my body still braces for one." Minor changes in tone or timing feel disproportionately significant. She sometimes withholds her feelings to avoid seeming "too much" or "too insecure," which builds tension and leads to emotional distance.

After a triggering weekend—Cole didn't reply to a message while out with friends—Rossilyn had a panic response and nearly ended the relationship. Instead, she brought the moment to therapy and began exploring the difference between intuitive concern and trauma-driven fear.

The Shift

Through therapy and open conversations with Cole, Rossilyn begins developing internal trust cues:

- She practices naming the emotion without assuming the worst: *"I feel anxious right now, but that doesn't mean something's wrong."*
- She uses grounding techniques when her thoughts spiral: body scanning, breathwork, or texting a trusted friend before confronting Cole.
- She commits to speaking from vulnerability rather than accusation: *"I know this is old fear showing up, but I want to talk through what I'm feeling."*

Cole, for his part, reassures with empathy rather than defensiveness. He says, "I know that someone else made trust feel unsafe. I want to build a new pattern with you—even if it takes time."

Where They Are Now

Rossilyn still experiences waves of uncertainty, especially during moments of distance or silence. But she no longer reacts impulsively or views Cole through the lens of her past. "I'm learning to let trust be something I build inside me, not something I demand from someone else," she writes in her journal.

Their relationship is a work in progress—but one marked by emotional courage, patience, and a shared commitment to healing.

How to Begin Reflecting

Self-reflection can start simply and easily, with a few deliberate questions asked in a quiet moment or written in a journal. The key is honesty, openness, and the willingness to sit with difficult emotions without rushing to resolve them.

Try starting with prompts like:

- What emotion am I feeling right now?
- What might have triggered this feeling?

- Have I felt this way before in similar situations?
- What do I need right now—support, space, comfort, clarity?
- What would a compassionate voice say to me in this moment?

Writing your answers down can reveal patterns over time. So can reflecting after emotionally charged events—whether it's a conflict with a partner, a stressful work meeting, or a moment of unexpected joy.

The Role of Mindfulness in Reflection

Mindfulness and self-reflection are complementary practices. While mindfulness trains you to observe your emotions in the present moment, reflection helps you make sense of those emotions over time. Together, they deepen your capacity to understand not just what you feel—but why.[38]

For example, mindfulness might help you notice that your chest tightens during conflict. Reflection might help you realize that this physical response began in childhood, when disagreement felt unsafe. That insight opens the door to healing and change.

Ritual of Self-Inquiry

Like any emotional skill, self-reflection deepens with practice.

Daily | Set aside 10-15 minutes at the end of your day to ask yourself:

- When did I feel most alive today?
- When did I feel most shut down or reactive?
- What can I learn from those moments?

Weekly | Use those 10-15 minutes to ask yourself:

- When was the last time I felt misunderstood?
- What did I need that I didn't know how to express?
- What emotion have I been avoiding lately—and why?
- In what ways am I still holding onto beliefs that no longer serve me?
- What's one pattern I keep repeating in my relationships, and what might it be trying to teach me?

Our goal with self-reflection is not to fix yourself, but to meet yourself. As you explore your emotional landscape with compassion, you learn to trust your inner world as a source of wisdom. And from that wisdom, you gain the power to choose differently, love more deeply, and live more authentically.

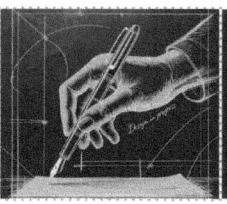

Reflection Prompts & Journaling Exercises by Attachment Style

SECURE ATTACHMENT

Reflection Prompts:

1. When I experience conflict with someone close to me, how do I typically respond?

2. How easy is it for me to express my needs, and how do others usually respond?

3. In what areas of my life do I feel emotionally safe and seen?

Journaling Exercises:

- Write about a time when you felt supported and emotionally connected to someone. What behaviors made that experience feel safe?

- List three ways you currently support others emotionally. How do you know when someone feels safe with you?

ANXIOUS ATTACHMENT

Reflection Prompts:

1. What situations trigger my fear of being abandoned or not being "enough"?

2. When I don't get immediate responses or validation, how do I feel—and what do I tend to do?

3. What would it feel like to trust someone without constant reassurance?

Journaling Exercises:

- Write a letter to your younger self during a time when you felt ignored or rejected. Reassure them using the words you most longed to hear.

- Track your internal responses during a recent moment of uncertainty in a relationship. Note the thoughts, emotions, and physical sensations that arose. Then rewrite the narrative using more compassionate or grounded language

AVOIDANT ATTACHMENT

Reflection Prompts:

1. When someone wants emotional closeness with me, what thoughts or discomforts arise?

2. How do I typically respond to vulnerability—my own or others'?

3. What would it feel like to need someone and still feel strong?

Journaling Exercises:

- Recall a time you withdrew emotionally. What were you protecting yourself from? What might you have needed but didn't ask for?

- Write about a relationship where closeness felt safe. If this feels difficult, explore why it might be hard to identify such a connection.

DISORGANIZED ATTACHMENT

Reflection Prompts:

1. Do I ever feel torn between wanting closeness and pushing people away?

2. What early experiences shaped my understanding of love and safety?

3. When I feel overwhelmed in a relationship, what part of me is trying to protect me—and what does it fear?

Journaling Exercises:

- Describe a moment when you felt both deeply connected and deeply afraid in a relationship. What was happening in your body, and how did you respond?

- Create a dialogue between your "attachment self" (the part that longs for love) and your "protective self" (the part that keeps people at arm's length). Let them speak to each other with curiosity, not judgment.

Inner Child Work: Healing Past Wounds

Beneath our adult behaviors and beliefs often lives a younger part of us—still holding the emotional residue of early experiences. This is the inner child: the emotional imprint of our past, shaped by the people and environments that first taught us about love, safety, and worth.

Inner child work reconnects us with that part of ourselves to begin healing emotional wounds that may have gone unacknowledged. By bringing awareness to the experiences that shaped our emotional development, we create the possibility of new responses and healthier patterns.

Why the Inner Child Matters

Even when we intellectually understand our behaviors, our emotional reactions can seem disproportionate. We may panic at the idea of being ignored, overreact to criticism, or shut down during conflict. These reactions often come from a much earlier version of us—a child who learned that certain situations, feelings, or needs were dangerous or unwelcome.[39]

When this younger self is ignored, emotional patterns become ingrained and often repeated. But when we approach those early wounds with compassion and curiosity, we shift from reenacting pain to transforming it.

Signs Your Inner Child Needs Healing

You struggle with abandonment fears or emotional reactivity in relationships

- You feel "not good enough" no matter how much you achieve
- You people-please, over-function, or fear setting boundaries

- You avoid vulnerability or equate love with performance
- You feel stuck in repeating patterns of sabotage, mistrust, or low self-worth

These are learned responses–survival strategies–not flaws. They helped you adapt to environments that didn't fully meet your emotional needs. Understanding them opens the door to healing.

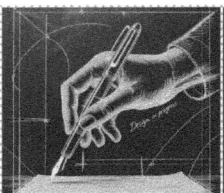

Inner Child Work Worksheet

Reconnect with the younger you who still lives inside. Offer them the love, safety, and validation they may not have received.

Step 1: Meet Your Inner Child

Close your eyes. Picture yourself at a specific age—somewhere between 4 and 10.

What do you see? Where are you? What's on your face, in your posture, in your eyes?

Describe your inner child in a few words or sentences.

Step 2: Identify Core Beliefs That Formed Early

As a child, you may have learned certain messages—directly or indirectly—from caregivers, culture, or early experiences.

What do you think this younger version of you believed about love, safety, or self-worth?

Check any that resonate or add your own:

- ☐ "I have to earn love by being good."
- ☐ "If I upset people, they'll leave."
- ☐ "My needs are too much."
- ☐ "I'm responsible for keeping peace."
- ☐ "No one really sees me."
- ☐ "I should stay quiet to stay safe."

Other:

Which of these beliefs still show up in your adult relationships—especially when you're stressed, triggered, or afraid?

Step 3: What Did Your Inner Child Need?

Go back to that younger version of yourself. Imagine sitting beside them.

What did they most need to hear, feel, or experience that they may not have received consistently?

- ☐ To be comforted when they were sad
- ☐ To be told they were loved just for existing
- ☐ To be protected from chaos or adult responsibilities
- ☐ To be seen and accepted for who they really were
- ☐ To be allowed to express big feelings

Other:

Step 4: Reparenting—Offer What Was Missing

Write a letter or message from your current adult self to your inner child.

Use compassionate, clear, nurturing language. Tell them what they needed to hear then—and what they may still long to hear now.

Begin with something like: "Hi sweetheart, I see you. You don't have to hold all of that anymore..."

Step 5: Integration—Bridging Past & Present

Your inner child still shows up in your adult life—especially in moments of fear, shame, or rejection. The difference now? You can show up for them.

The next time I feel triggered or overwhelmed, I will…

- ☐ Pause and check in with my inner child: "What are you afraid of right now?"
- ☐ Offer comfort: "You're not alone. I've got you."
- ☐ Gently remind myself: "This feeling is old. I'm safe now."
- ☐ Other:

Affirmation for Your Inner Child

Choose or create one:

- ☐ "You were never too much. You were just too much for people who hadn't done their own healing."
- ☐ "You didn't deserve what happened—and it's not your fault."
- ☐ "You are deeply lovable. Even when you're sad. Even when you're scared."
- ☐ "You're safe with me now."
- ☐ Other:

Final Reflection

What do you want your inner child to know today?

Reminder: Healing isn't about erasing the past. It's about becoming the safe, loving presence you always deserved—and can now offer yourself.

BONUS: Partner Conversation Starter

"I came across a reflection exercise that invites us to explore how our childhood experiences shaped the way we connect in relationships now—not to blame the past, but to understand ourselves and each other more deeply. Want to do it together and talk about what comes up for each of us?"

Bonus Prompt for Shared Reflection:

"What's something your younger self needed to hear that they didn't? What would it mean for me to say it to you now?"

Foundational Practices in Inner Child Healing

1. Visualization

Create a quiet, supportive space. Picture yourself as a child—perhaps at a time when you felt unseen or vulnerable. Notice their expression, posture, and energy. Sit with this image and offer words of care: *You're safe now. You are lovable. It wasn't your fault.* Even if it feels awkward at first, this compassionate reconnection can begin to repair emotional ruptures.[40]

2. Letter Writing

Write to your younger self from the perspective of your present-day self. Express the compassion, comfort, and reassurance that may have been missing at the time. Let the letter affirm what that child needed to hear—messages that can begin to reshape your inner narrative.

3. Reparenting Practices

Reparenting is the act of caring for your emotional needs in ways that support growth and safety. If you needed comfort as a child, practice self-soothing now. If you needed protection, set firm boundaries. This is how you become the stable, nurturing presence your inner child has been waiting for.

4. Trigger Awareness

Notice when you feel particularly sensitive, irrational, or reactive. Ask yourself: *What age does this version of me feel like? What did I need then that I'm still searching for now?* Self-awareness is the bridge between reactivity and healing.[41]

Acknowledging Grief and Moving Forward

Healing may stir up emotions that were long buried—grief, anger, confusion. You might mourn the love you wished for or the safety that was never available. Giving yourself permission to feel these emotions is part of the healing process. It allows you to reclaim the emotional space that once felt unsafe.

Forgiveness may or may not feature in your journey. What matters more is letting go of the past so you can move more freely in the present.

Inner child work addresses our stuck parts by revisiting the past where wounds first formed. When you reconnect with a part of yourself that was silenced or ignored, you give voice to the truth that has always wanted to be heard: you are worthy. You're whole. You're no longer alone.

Embracing Vulnerability: The Courage to Connect Embracing Emotional Openness

Armor can feel fantastic. It can make mushy parts of yourself impenetrable and give you plenty of courage in seemingly dangerous situations. Guarding up blocks all kinds of potential threats from coming in.

It also blocks anything from going out. Including, and especially, *you*.

Vulnerability often feels like standing in the open without armor—uncertain, exposed, and at risk of rejection. Yet it's through these moments of openness that we form our deepest connections. Vulnerability is the doorway to emotional intimacy, trust, and authenticity. Without it, relationships remain surface-level, guarded by performance and self-protection.

Many people's fear of vulnerability stems from their early experiences. Perhaps openness resulted in criticism, betrayal, or indifference. Over time, the mind begins to associate emotional exposure with danger. We become adept at concealing our emotions—masking pain with humor, avoiding difficult conversations, or over-functioning in the hope that being needed will feel safer than being seen.

This fear is understandable. Vulnerability involves risk. It also allows for genuine closeness, which cannot be manufactured through perfection or control. When we allow ourselves to be seen in our imperfection, we give others permission to do the same.

To open up emotionally, it's important to first recognize how you guard yourself. Common protective behaviors include:

- Deflecting with sarcasm or humor
- Shutting down during emotional conversations
- Overanalyzing instead of feeling
- Seeking approval through overachievement
- Avoiding intimacy by staying busy or distracted

These strategies serve a purpose: they offer safety. The goal isn't to eliminate them overnight, but to grow curious about when and why they appear. That curiosity creates the space to make more conscious choices.

Case Study: Priya's Journey Toward Vulnerability

Background:

Priya (she/her), a 34-year-old woman of Indian heritage, had long been known in her family as the dependable one. As the eldest daughter, she carried unspoken expectations: excel academically, build a respected career, and uphold the family's reputation. Growing up, emotions like fear, sadness, or anger were rarely voiced openly at home. If Priya felt overwhelmed, her parents reminded her of resilience—

"These feelings will pass, focus on your work." Love was conveyed more through acts of care—hot meals, financial support, sacrifices—than through emotional conversations.

The Situation

Now married to Ravi (he/him), who also came from a close-knit Indian family, Priya continued to carry that invisible armor. Their relationship was strong in many ways: they shared cultural traditions, cooked together on weekends, and regularly visited extended family. But when it came to expressing deeper feelings, Priya often retreated. If disagreements arose, she kept her voice even, sometimes offering practical solutions but rarely saying how she truly felt. She feared being "too much"—too emotional, too needy—and worried that Ravi might lose respect for her if she exposed her softer side.

Ravi, on the other hand, longed for more openness. Though raised in a household where emotions were not often spoken aloud, he had gradually learned, through therapy and his own reflection, the importance of emotional connection. One evening after dinner, he gently said to her, *"Priya, I feel like I know everything about your day, your plans, your goals—but I don't always know how you feel. I want to know that part of you, too."*

His words unsettled her. In her mind, she was already doing so much—managing work deadlines, helping her parents with errands, and making sure family expectations were met. Wasn't that enough? But later that night, Priya sat quietly with his request. She realized she had mistaken efficiency and steadiness for intimacy. She was present in action but hidden in emotion.

The Shift

A week later, during a morning walk with Ravi, she tried something different. Her heart raced as she said, *"Sometimes I feel anxious when I can't hold everything together—at work, with our families, even with us. I'm afraid you'll think I'm weak if I admit that."* The words felt raw, unpolished, and terrifying to release.

Ravi paused, then reached for her hand. *"Priya, I don't see you as weak. I see you as human. And it makes me feel closer to you when you let me in."*

That moment stayed with her. Later, she journaled about how naming her fear— *"I'm afraid of being seen as weak"* —gave it less power. She noticed that sharing even a small truth had not caused distance; instead, it created closeness.

The Outcome:

Over the next few months, Priya practiced vulnerability in other ways: telling Ravi when she felt overwhelmed by balancing extended family obligations, admitting when she needed rest instead of hosting guests, and letting him see her cry without brushing it off. Each time felt risky, but each time, Ravi met her with empathy rather than judgment.

For Priya, vulnerability became a bridge. It did not erase her sense of responsibility or her cultural values of family devotion and resilience. Instead, it deepened her marriage, allowing her and Ravi to honor tradition while also creating space for emotional intimacy. By letting her armor down piece by piece, Priya discovered that true strength was not in never wavering—it was in being seen and loved even when she did.

Steps Toward Emotional Openness

1. Start with Safe People

Choose someone you trust—someone who listens without fixing, who responds with empathy. Share something small. Then pause. Notice how it feels to be met, not managed.

2. Name the Fear

Rather than pushing through discomfort, acknowledge it. You might say, *"This feels hard to share,"* or *"I'm afraid this might change how you see me."* Naming the fear softens its grip.

3. Share Emotions, Not Explanations

Try saying, *"I feel overwhelmed,"* instead of *"I've just been really busy with work."* Focus on the experience, not the defense. Emotional truth builds trust more than polished stories ever can.

4. Practice Self-Compassion

Opening up is a risk, even with supportive people. If you feel exposed afterward, tend to yourself gently. Remind yourself that discomfort doesn't mean you did something wrong; it means you did something brave.

Emotional openness isn't about spilling everything at once; it's about learning to be present with your truth and trusting that it matters. As you practice vulnerability, you will notice a shift in your interactions with others and with yourself. What was once fragile now feels like strength.

Building Emotional Resilience: Strategies for Growth

Emotional resilience is your ability to adapt, recover, and grow through emotional difficulty. It won't spare you from feeling overwhelmed or shaken—it means you've developed the inner strength to navigate challenges without losing your sense of self. Like a tree that bends in the storm without breaking, resilience allows you to stay rooted even when life gets turbulent.

Imagine receiving unexpected criticism at work. Without resilience, you risk spiraling into self-doubt or becoming defensive. With resilience, you pause. You breathe. You acknowledge the sting without allowing it to define you. Then you reflect: *Is there anything I can learn here? What do I want to do next that is consistent with who I am?* You will continue to feel discomfort, but it will now be beneficial to your growth.

Some people associate resilience with toughness or stoicism, but true resilience is flexible, not rigid. It includes self-awareness, emotional agility, healthy coping, and the ability to draw support when needed.

Everyone experiences emotional stress—loss, disappointment, conflict, uncertainty.

Resilience helps you:

- Bounce back from emotional setbacks
- Respond rather than react in stressful situations
- Adapt to change while preserving your core values
- Maintain optimism and purpose during trying times

Research shows that emotionally resilient individuals tend to have better mental health outcomes, stronger relationships, and greater satisfaction with life.[43] Pain doesn't have to be avoided or feared when we can trust in our ability to move through it. Resilience transforms the threat of pain into opportunity.

Core Strategies for Building Resilience

1. Name Your Emotions Without Judgment

Self-awareness is the foundation of emotional intelligence and the first step toward resilience. When you can identify what you're feeling—grief, frustration, fear, loneliness—you reduce emotional chaos. Practice asking yourself, *What am I feeling right now?* and *What might this feeling be trying to show me?* Emotional labeling activates regions in the brain associated with regulation and reduces stress reactivity.[44]

2. Practice Self-Compassion

Many people respond to pain by turning against themselves. But berating yourself doesn't make you stronger—it makes you smaller. Instead, respond to your struggles as you would to a friend: with kindness, support, and encouragement. Self-compassion has been shown to improve emotional regulation and reduce anxiety and depression.[45]

Try this simple practice: Place your hand over your heart and say to yourself, *This is a difficult moment. It's okay to feel this way. I'm here for myself.*

3. Build a Toolbox of Coping Skills

Effective coping doesn't mean pushing through at all costs—it means knowing what restores your energy. Your toolbox might include:

- Deep breathing or grounding techniques
- Physical activity or movement
- Connecting with someone you trust
- Creative expression (writing, music, art)
- Time in nature or calming spaces

Experiment to find what helps you reconnect with your center—and make those tools part of your daily rhythm.

4. Develop Cognitive Flexibility

Rigid thinking—*This will never get better,* or *I can't handle this*—can make stress feel insurmountable. Resilience grows when you challenge those thoughts and replace them with more balanced perspectives: *This is hard, and I've gotten through hard things before.* This shift helps reduce catastrophizing and opens space for hope and action.[46]

5. Strengthen Meaning and Purpose

People who feel connected to something larger than themselves—whether it's a personal mission, faith, creativity, or community—tend to recover more quickly from emotional adversity. Purpose gives suffering a context. Ask yourself: *What matters most to me right now? What values can guide me through this challenge?*

Resilience is a skill set you can develop, not a static trait.[42] Resilience is built in everyday moments—in how you speak to yourself after failure, how you show up when life is messy, and how you keep going, even when things feel uncertain. You don't have to always be okay; you can choose to always believe that you'll find your way, even when you're not.

Reflection Journal: Practicing Growth Mindset in Relationships

Love is not about always getting it right. It's about being willing to keep showing up differently—when we know better, when we feel more, and when we're ready to grow.

Step 1: Rethink Mistakes

Think of a recent moment in a relationship where you felt misunderstood, criticized, or defensive. Describe it briefly below:

What was your first instinct in that moment?
- ☐ Withdraw
- ☐ Defend yourself
- ☐ Shut down emotionally
- ☐ Criticize back
- ☐ Other:

Step 2: Reframe the Moment

What would it have looked like to approach that moment with a growth mindset? (e.g., "I don't have to get this perfect—I can try again," or "This is feedback, not failure.")

If you could rewind and respond from a place of curiosity instead of fear, what might you have said or done differently?

Step 3: What Are You Learning About...

Yourself in relationships?

What triggers you—and why?

How you want to show up moving forward?

Step 4: Create a Growth-Oriented Script

Choose one of the following phrases to try during your next conflict—or create your own:

- "I didn't get that right, but I want to learn."
- "This is hard for me, and I'm trying to stay present."
- "Can we try that conversation again?"
- "I see now how that hurt you—I wasn't aware in the moment."

Your own:

Affirmation for Connection

"We don't have to be perfect to be loved.

"We just have to be willing to grow."

03

Cultivating Healthy Relationships

For the first time in a long time, Paul was giving me space. Space to say what was real. Space to let the words leave my body and land between us. I wasn't going to waste it.

"Worst-case scenario looks like separation. Divorce. Coparenting."

His eyes widened. His mouth parted, just slightly, like the wind had been knocked out of him. For me, the answer felt so obvious I almost didn't think it needed saying. But the expression on his face told me otherwise.

I braced for the usual response—defensiveness, deflection, accusations. That had been his pattern. Mine too, in different ways.

But instead of rising, he folded.

His shoulders curved inward. The corners of his mouth dropped. His brow knit with something like sorrow. A thin shimmer of emotion glazed his eyes as he searched mine again.

When he spoke, his voice was soft, raw in a way I hadn't heard in years.

"I don't want that."

My own throat tightened. I felt my emotions rising to meet his. There, on his face, was something we'd both been too defensive to show for too long: vulnerability. And knowing my words had touched that place in him, it landed like a battering ram to my chest.

"I don't either," I whispered back.

For a moment, we were quiet. But it wasn't the usual silence of avoidance. It was a pause that held weight. Potential.

"Then what do we do?" he asked.

That question—simple as it was—signaled a shift.

It wasn't just about whether we would stay together. It was about *how* we would show up for each other, and whether we could learn to relate in new, healthier ways.

We had spent so long reacting from wounded places—talking past each other, guarding ourselves, performing roles instead of expressing needs. But in that moment, something cracked open. We weren't solving everything. But we were starting to talk. To really *communicate*.

The truth is that love isn't sustained by good intentions alone.

It requires communication that's mindful and clear.

It requires trust that is built, broken, and rebuilt.

It requires understanding what intimacy really looks like—and how to balance closeness with individuality.

It asks us to learn the language of the people we love, and to navigate conflict as a doorway, not a dead end.

That's where we turned next. And that's where this chapter begins.

Effective Communication: Bridging Emotional Gaps

Every relationship has moments of misalignment—times when what's said doesn't match what's heard, or when silence grows louder than words. These emotional gaps can quietly widen over time, creating distance between people who genuinely care about each other. Effective communication is how we bridge those spaces. It's how we create mutual understanding, validate emotional experiences, and restore connection when things feel strained.

Communication is more than words. It's tone, timing, body language, and intent. It's how we listen, how we respond, and how we manage our own emotional states during moments of stress or misunderstanding. Often, conflict arises not because people don't care, but because they're struggling to feel heard or understood.[50]

The Core Functions of Communication in Relationships

At its heart, effective communication serves three essential functions:

1. **Connection**—It allows us to share feelings, needs, and desires.
2. **Clarity**—It helps us articulate thoughts in ways that minimize misinterpretation.
3. **Repair**—It becomes the pathway for reconnection after rupture, fostering trust and resilience.

Couples and close partners who communicate well can navigate conflict with intention. They recognize that communication is an emotional exchange, not just an exchange of information.[51]

Common Barriers to Connection

Even with the best intentions, communication can go awry. Common pitfalls include:

- **Assumptions** ("They should already know how I feel")
- **Mind reading** ("If they cared, they'd act differently without me asking")
- **Defensiveness** (reacting with justification instead of curiosity)
- **Stonewalling** (withdrawing emotionally to avoid discomfort)[52]

These habits often develop as protective responses, especially when past communication efforts were met with criticism or neglect. Unpacking them requires both self-awareness and a willingness to shift from blame to collaboration.

(Note: Shifting from blame to collaboration can be hard. It's one thing to read it in a book, but wholly different in practice. We blame when we feel unsafe to be wrong. When you learn to have your own back unconditionally, you can trust you'll survive being wrong. When you're open to being wrong, you're able to collaborate. Doing this automatically in tense moments takes *a lot* of practice. Every attempt to shift, even if it's messy, builds the habit. So, go easy on yourself in the moment, and keep trying.)

Foundational Skills for Effective Communication

1. Clear, Direct Language
Express needs without layering them in sarcasm, guilt, or ambiguity. Instead of *"I guess you're too busy for me again,"* try *"I'd really appreciate some time together tonight. Can we plan for that?"*

2. Emotionally Honest Statements
Use "I feel" statements that name your emotions without assigning blame. For example: *"I feel disconnected when we don't talk about what's bothering us."*

3. Reflective Listening
After someone shares, respond with a simple reflection: *"It sounds like you felt overwhelmed today."* This doesn't mean you agree—it means you understand.

4. Regulated Timing
Communicate difficult things when both people are emotionally available. A calm nervous system is a better listener than a flooded one.

Effective communication is a skill, not a trait, and it's one that can be practiced every day. Whether you're expressing appreciation or addressing a conflict, how you show up in conversation becomes the foundation of emotional safety. Over time, these daily exchanges can accumulate into a relationship that feels strong, responsive, and deeply connected.

Conversation Practice Guide: Building Connection Through Everyday Dialogue

This guide helps couples or close partners practice communication in low-stakes moments, so they're better prepared for emotionally charged ones. Use it regularly—during a walk, over dinner, or before bed.

Step 1: Choose a Calm Moment

Only engage in this practice when both people feel emotionally available and not in the middle of conflict or stress

Step 2: Use the "Check-In + Listen" Format

Each partner takes 2–3 minutes to answer one of the following prompts. The other person listens silently, offering full presence (no interrupting, no problem-solving).

Sample Prompts:

- "Today I felt most connected when..."
- "Something I've been carrying emotionally this week is..."
- "One thing I appreciated about you recently is..."
- "Something I'm looking forward to is..."
- "One thing I need more of in our relationship right now is..."

When both partners have shared, reflect briefly:

- "What I heard you say was..."
- "That makes sense. Thank you for telling me."

This is not a debate or decision-making conversation—it's about creating safety and understanding.

Step 3: Practice Emotional Naming

When emotions come up, name them clearly:
- "I felt sad/disconnected/proud/hopeful when..."
- "That reminded me of a feeling I've had before in other moments..."
- "I didn't know how to say it at the time, but I was feeling..."

Even if your partner doesn't fully relate to your experience, emotional naming invites empathy and lowers defensiveness.

Step 4: Regroup Later If Needed

Sometimes conversations open up deeper territory. You don't need to solve everything in one sitting. Try:
- "Can we come back to this tomorrow? I want to give it more space."
- "Let's sit with what we've shared for now—I'm glad we're talking."

Partner Reflection Prompts: Strengthening Emotional Understanding

Use these journal-style prompts individually or discuss them together during a quiet moment. They're designed to deepen empathy, awareness, and emotional insight.

For Individual Reflection:

1. When do I feel most emotionally connected to my partner?
2. What makes it hard for me to express vulnerability in conversations?
3. How do I tend to react when I feel misunderstood or dismissed?
4. What do I most appreciate about the way my partner communicates with me?
5. What's one thing I want to express more openly in our relationship?

For Shared Conversation:

1. What does feeling "heard" look like for each of us?
2. How can we tell when the other person is overwhelmed, and what helps in those moments?
3. What patterns do we notice in how we approach conflict—and what would we like to shift?
4. Are there topics we avoid because they feel difficult? What would help us approach them more openly?
5. How can we make space for more daily check-ins that feel meaningful, even when we're busy?

Mindful Communication Techniques

Let's welcome mindfulness back to the stage.

Communication in close relationships is more than simply exchanging information; it is an ongoing opportunity to connect, affirm, and understand. When stress or emotions are high, we frequently engage in reactive behaviors such as interrupting, zoning out, defending, or assuming. Mindful communication returns us to presence. It allows us to slow down, regulate our emotions, and intentionally interact with others, even during stressful situations.

Mindfulness in communication begins with awareness—noticing what's happening in your body, mind, and emotions as you engage with someone else. Instead of rushing to respond or retreating into your thoughts, you stay grounded in the moment. This shift can change the entire tone of a conversation. [33]

Core Principles of Mindful Communication

1. Presence Over Performance
Mindful communication starts with showing up fully. That means letting go of rehearsed responses, multitasking, or jumping ahead in the conversation. When you're truly present, the other person feels it. Presence communicates safety, which is the foundation of trust.[36]

2. Listening to Understand
Instead of preparing your next point while the other person is talking, focus on understanding their experience. Pay attention to their words, tone, and body language. When they finish speaking, try reflecting back what you heard:

- "It sounds like you felt unheard in that moment."
- "I'm hearing that this really mattered to you."

This reflective language signals empathy without assuming agreement.

3. Speaking with Intention

Mindful speaking means expressing your thoughts and feelings clearly, without blame or exaggeration. Use "I" statements that focus on your emotional experience:

- "I felt anxious when I didn't hear from you yesterday."
- "I feel more connected when we check in at the end of the day."

Avoid generalizations like "you always" or "you never," which tend to trigger defensiveness.

4. Regulating Your Nervous System

When communication becomes emotionally charged, it's easy to move into fight, flight, freeze, or fawn mode. Mindful communicators notice the signs of activation—racing heart, shallow breath, tension—and use tools like deep breathing or gentle grounding (placing both feet on the floor, pausing before speaking) to stay present.[54]

5. Creating Space to Pause

Silence is a powerful tool. Taking a breath before responding can prevent knee-jerk reactions and allow for more thoughtful, compassionate replies. If needed, name the pause:

- "I'm thinking about how I want to respond to that."
- "Can we take a few minutes and come back to this?"

Mindful communication softens the edges of conflict. It turns confrontations into opportunities for closeness. With regular practice, even difficult moments become invitations to grow stronger together.

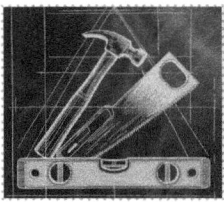

Mindful Communication Practice Guide

Mindful communication brings awareness to both what we say and how we say it. This guide will help you slow down, stay emotionally present, and respond from clarity rather than habit

Step 1: Ground Yourself Before Speaking

Before entering a vulnerable or important conversation, pause. Take 2–3 deep breaths. Notice:

- Your posture
- Your emotional state
- Your intention for the conversation

Ask yourself: Am I here to connect, to control, or to be right

Step 2: Practice Conscious Speaking

When speaking, use language that is:

- Specific: Describe feelings and needs clearly.
- Non-blaming: Avoid "you never" or "you always."
- Emotionally honest: Use "I feel…" followed by the emotion, not an accusation.

Try this format (inspired by Nonviolent Communication):

> "When [situation] happened, I felt [emotion] because I needed [value/need]. Would you be willing to [specific request]?"

Example:
"When we didn't talk last night, I felt lonely because I really value connection before bed. Could we make time to talk tonight?"

Step 3: Practice Conscious Listening

Mindful listening means:
- Maintaining eye contact
- Avoiding interruptions
- Focusing on understanding rather than fixing

After your partner finishes speaking, pause before responding. Then try:
- "I hear that you're feeling…"
- "It sounds like this mattered to you because…"
- "I'm glad you told me that."

This slows the pace of conversation and fosters emotional attunement.

Step 4: Take Breaks When Flooded

If you feel emotionally overwhelmed, it's okay to pause. Try saying:

> "I care about this conversation and want to stay present. Can we take a short break and come back to it?"

Then engage in a calming practice (deep breathing, movement, solitude) before resuming.

Partner Reflection Prompts: Exploring Mindfulness in Communication

Use these prompts to reflect individually or discuss together. They help uncover communication patterns and build awareness of how presence (or absence) impacts the relationship.

For Individual Reflection

1. What physical or emotional cues tell me I'm becoming reactive during a conversation?
2. When do I find it hardest to stay present while listening?
3. What topics or emotions do I tend to avoid—and why?
4. How do I feel after speaking mindfully? How does it differ from reacting automatically?
5. What's one communication habit I'd like to change or strengthen?

For Shared Conversation

1. How can we help each other stay present and grounded during difficult conversations?
2. What helps each of us feel heard and understood?
3. How do we tend to respond when one of us gets emotionally overwhelmed—and what might work better?
4. What mindful rituals could we use to reconnect during the day (e.g., device-free meals, daily check-ins)?
5. How does our pace of communication affect how connected we feel?

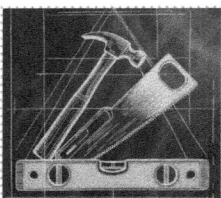

Nonverbal Behaviors & What They May Reveal Emotionally

Remember nonverbal communication is a two-way interaction—you display as much as you receive. Practice the nonverbal behavior you wish to display in your conversations, then bring mindfulness to your own body in a conversation to help support your intention and your words.

Eye Contact

- Sustained, warm eye contact → Interest, affection, connection
- Avoiding eye contact → Shame, guilt, disconnection, anxiety
- Staring intensely → Anger, confrontation, dominance
- Frequent blinking or darting eyes → Nervousness, insecurity, fear

Posture

- Open posture (uncrossed arms, facing forward) → Receptiveness, safety, calm
- Turned away body or leaning back → Discomfort, disengagement, disapproval
- Rigid, upright posture → Defensiveness, alertness, control
- Slouched or collapsed posture → Sadness, fatigue, defeat

Gestures & Movement

- Gentle, fluid hand gestures → Calm, confidence, empathy
- Fidgeting or restless movements → Anxiety, overwhelm, impatience
- Pointing or jabbing → Anger, aggression, dominance
- Hands covering face/mouth → Embarrassment, hesitation, fear

Facial Expressions
- Soft eyes + slight smile → Compassion, warmth, presence
- Tight jaw or clenched teeth → Anger, stress, holding back emotion
- •Raised eyebrows → Surprise, disbelief, curiosity
- Furrowed brow → Confusion, concern, frustration
- Blank expression → Emotional withdrawal, masking emotion, overwhelm

Tone of Voice (Paraverbal Cues)
- Soft, steady voice → Safety, comfort, empathy
- Raised pitch or volume → Excitement, anxiety, urgency, or anger
- Flat or monotone voice → Disinterest, depression, shutdown
- Frequent hesitations or trailing off → Uncertainty, shame, vulnerability

Proximity & Touch
- Leaning in or touching lightly → Intimacy, trust, warmth
- Physical distance or stepping back → Discomfort, boundary-setting, fear
- Sudden withdrawal of touch → Hurt, anger, betrayal
- Lingering hugs or hand-holding → Reassurance, safety, love

Note to Readers:

Nonverbal communication is not always universal—context matters. But learning to observe body language with curiosity (rather than assumption) can help you better understand your partner's emotional landscape—and your own.

From Conflict to Connection: A Mindful Communication Worksheet

Turn small moments of tension into deeper understanding using emotional intelligence tools

Step 1: Identify the Trigger Moment

What was the surface issue? (e.g., dishes in the sink, forgotten text, tone of voice)

What emotion did it trigger in you first?

- ☐ Frustration
- ☐ Hurt
- ☐ Rejection
- ☐ Disrespect
- ☐ Guilt
- ☐ Something else:

What story did your mind start telling you in that moment?

(e.g., "They don't appreciate me," "I'm doing everything alone," "I can't say anything without a fight")

Step 2: Pause & Regulate

Before responding, try one of these regulating tools:

- ☐ Take 3 deep breaths
- ☐ Put a hand on your heart or belly
- ☐ Step away for a moment (with a promise to return)
- ☐ Say to yourself: "This is hard, but I can respond with care."

Step 3: Express with "I Feel" + Vulnerability

Use this sentence frame to express your inner world without blame:

"When _____ happened, I felt _____ because I was needing _____."

"What I wish for is _____."

Example:

"When I saw the dishes, I felt overwhelmed because I was needing support. What I wish for is to feel like we're in this together."

Now, write your own:

Step 4: Practice Active Listening

If your partner is speaking:
- Make eye contact
- Reflect back what you heard ("So what I'm hearing is…")
- Ask: "Did I get that right?"
- Validate the emotion before problem-solving
- Avoid defensiveness or rebuttals

Write down one thing your partner shared that surprised or touched you:

Step 5: Reconnect Intentionally

Use one of these repair tools to close the loop:

- ☐ "Thank you for telling me how you feel."
- ☐ "I see where I hurt you—and that wasn't my intention."
- ☐ "I want to do better. Let's figure out how together."
- ☐ "I care more about us than being right."
- ☐ Your own:

Reflection: What Did You Learn?

- What was really underneath the argument?
- What helped you shift from reacting to connecting?
- What would you like to remember next time you feel triggered?

Reminder: You don't need perfect communication to build connection—you just need consistent courage, curiosity, and care.

Building Trust: Overcoming Past Hurts

Trust is the emotional backbone of any lasting relationship. It gives us the safety to show up fully, share openly, and lean on each other in moments of uncertainty. But for many, trust doesn't come easily—especially when past experiences have included betrayal, neglect, or emotional inconsistency.

Healing from relational wounds takes time, intention, and vulnerability. Trust doesn't automatically repair with an apology or the passage of time. It's rebuilt through repeated, small moments of consistency, accountability, and emotional attunement.[51]

Case Study: Rebuilding After the Breakdown—Marcus and Dani

Background:

Marcus (38, he/him) and Dani (35, she/her) have been together for six years and married for three. In the early stages of their relationship, Marcus felt emotionally secure—Dani was consistent, present, and open. But two years into their marriage, Dani had an emotional entanglement with a coworker that she initially hid. Though there was no physical affair, Marcus discovered flirtatious texts that left him feeling betrayed and destabilized.

The Impact:

For Marcus, the rupture was profound. His emotional safety vanished overnight. He began double-checking Dani's phone habits, withdrew sexually, and found himself questioning every moment of connection: *Is she being honest? Am I being naive again?* Even small miscommunications—like Dani being late without texting—would trigger spiraling fears.

Dani, meanwhile, felt shame for her behavior but also frustration. She believed she had "come clean," ended the inappropriate connection, and wanted to move forward. She didn't understand why her efforts weren't enough to "earn back" Marcus's trust.

They entered therapy six months after the rupture, both unsure if the relationship could be salvaged.

The Turning Point

In their third session, the therapist invited each partner to explore what trust meant to them—not as an abstract ideal, but as a lived experience. Marcus shared, "Trust used to feel like ease. I didn't have to scan the room for danger. Now, even when you're kind, I feel tension in my chest."

That moment changed something for Dani. Instead of defending herself, she leaned in. "I think I've been treating your hurt like a countdown clock. I've been trying to do enough, fast enough, to make it stop. But I see now—it's not about proving I'm good. It's about helping you feel safe again."

Together, they began working on rebuilding through daily micro-moments:

- **Consistency:** Dani sent midday check-ins when working late or traveling.
- **Transparency:** She offered access to her phone—not as punishment, but as reassurance.
- **Repair efforts:** When trust wobbled, she didn't withdraw or blame; she said, "I understand why this feels hard."
- **Dani's part:** He practiced distinguishing past fear from present evidence, using grounding techniques when triggered. He also began voicing his emotions in real-time rather than shutting down.

Where They Are Now

One year later, Marcus and Dani still occasionally revisit the pain of that time—but it no longer defines their connection. Marcus shares that he feels "increasingly anchored" in the relationship. Dani describes their intimacy as "deeper, because it's real—we've seen each other at our worst and chosen to stay present."

Their story isn't about a perfect recovery. It's about how trust can slowly return when both people meet pain with accountability, presence, and empathy.

Why Past Hurts Resurface

Our nervous systems remember. Even long after a painful experience, the brain can remain on alert for signs of danger. A missed call, a shift in tone, or a broken promise may trigger past pain—even when it doesn't reflect current reality. These responses are adaptive strategies rooted in survival.[55]

If you've been hurt in the past, you may find yourself:

- Waiting for the other shoe to drop
- Withholding vulnerability out of self-protection
- Doubting your instincts or questioning your worth
- Reacting with anger or withdrawal even when the current situation is safe

These patterns are understandable—but they can also interfere with the growth of new, healthier relationships.

How Trust is Rebuilt

1. Name the Wound with Compassion

Healing begins with acknowledgment. Whether you've been hurt by a past partner, a caregiver, or within your current relationship, naming the impact allows it to be held and processed. Shame thrives in secrecy; healing begins in truth.

Try saying:

- "That experience left me questioning my worth."
- "It still feels hard to trust when things feel uncertain."
- "I want to rebuild trust, but I'm scared."

2. Rebuild with Action, Not Assumptions

Trust isn't rebuilt through promises, but through behavior. That includes:

- Following through on commitments
- Communicating clearly and consistently

- Creating emotional safety through listening, validation, and reliability
- Repairing after ruptures

Even one small act of reliability can begin to shift what once felt impossible to restore.[50]

3. Allow Time and Transparency

Restoring trust doesn't follow a set timeline. Be honest about what you need—whether that's more reassurance, more time, or more dialogue. Trust grows in environments where both people are committed to growth, not perfection.

4. Learn to Trust Yourself Again

Often, rebuilding external trust starts with internal trust. When you begin to trust your own voice, boundaries, and emotional intuition, you become more equipped to discern when a relationship feels truly safe.

Trust is not a static state—it's a relationship discipline. It is built and rebuilt in moments of presence, honesty, and repair. Even when trust has been broken, healing is possible. And when it's restored, it becomes stronger because both people chose to meet the rupture with courage, care, and accountability.

Trust-Building Exercise: "Across the Bridge"

A guided connection ritual to foster safety, empathy, and presence between two people.

Set the Space
- Sit facing each other in a quiet, comfortable environment
- Put phones away; make eye contact optional, but encouraged
- Breathe deeply for a few seconds before beginning

Part 1: "Getting to Know the Inner Landscape" (5–10 min each)

Take turns answering the following three prompts while the other listens silently—no interruptions, no fixing, just listening.

Speaker's Prompts:
1. "One thing I'm afraid to need from others is…"
2. "Something I long to feel in this relationship is…"
3. "What helps me feel safe when I'm struggling is…"

Optional: Add a hand on the heart or brief pause after each prompt to let the words land.

Listener's Role:
- Stay silent. Nod or show warmth, but don't respond until prompted.
- After the speaker is done, respond with:

"Thank you for trusting me with that. What I heard was…"
   (Then gently reflect what you understood. End with:)
      "Did I get it right?"

Switch roles after completing all three prompts.

Part 2: "The Bridge"—A Mutual Check-In (5–10 min)

Now work together to answer the following prompts:

1. "What's one small moment recently when I felt closer to you?"
2. "What's one thing I want to do more often to support our trust?"
3. "How do I tend to pull away when I'm hurt—and how can I let you in instead?"

Share honestly. Allow space for imperfection. Focus on curiosity over control.

Part 3: A Ritual of Repair and Reassurance

To close the exercise, each person completes this sentence:

"Even when things feel hard between us, I want you to know that I am still here, and I still care."

End with one of the following:

- ☐ A hug
- ☐ Eye contact and a shared breath
- ☐ Holding hands
- ☐ A shared silence

Optional Reflection Prompts (Journaling or Verbal)

- What was vulnerable or surprising in this conversation?
- What do I want to remember about my partner's emotional needs?
- How did I feel before, during, and after this exercise?

BONUS:
Partner Conversation Starter

"I've been thinking about how we connect—and how trust isn't just built in big moments, but in small ones where we really *see* each other. There's a simple exercise I came across that's not about fixing anything, just understanding each other more deeply.

Would you be open to trying it with me sometime soon? We'd take turns answering a few prompts and really listening without interruption. No pressure—just curiosity, presence, and us. I think it could help us feel closer."

Alternate versions (tailored by partner temperament):

For a logical or task-oriented partner:

"I found a short relationship exercise that's structured and only takes 20–30 minutes. It's designed to build trust through clearer communication. Would you be open to trying it with me sometime this week?"

For a partner who's been hurt or guarded:

"There's this gentle trust-building exercise I'd love to try with you. It's not heavy—it's about understanding each other, not digging up the past. We can go slow and stop anytime, but I think it might help us feel safer together."

For a growth-minded partner:

"I know we've been working on deepening our connection. There's a reflective practice we could do that helps build trust and emotional safety. It's just a few prompts and space to really listen to each other. Want to try it together?"

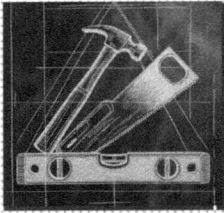
Trust-Building Habits Checklist

Small, consistent actions that strengthen emotional safety and connection.

1. Communication Habits

- ☐ I listen to understand, not just to respond
- ☐ I ask clarifying questions instead of making assumptions
- ☐ I express my feelings with honesty and care
- ☐ I share my needs without guilt or blame
- ☐ I follow through on what I say I'll do

2. Emotional Availability

- ☐ I make time to connect without distractions (phones off, eyes up)
- ☐ I acknowledge and validate my partner's emotions, even if I don't agree
- ☐ I offer comfort when my partner is hurting or overwhelmed
- ☐ I share my own vulnerabilities (fears, hopes, doubts)
- ☐ I stay present when conversations feel emotionally charged

3. Conflict Repair Skills

- ☐ I can say "I was wrong" or "I hurt you" without defensiveness
- ☐ I apologize sincerely and ask how to make things right
- ☐ I seek resolution, not just relief from discomfort
- ☐ I take breaks if needed—but always return to the conversation
- ☐ I prioritize the relationship over being right

4. Consistency & Reliability

- ☐ I show up when I say I will
- ☐ I keep personal information shared with me private
- ☐ I follow through on promises, even small ones
- ☐ I act in alignment with my words
- ☐ I create routines or rituals that reinforce emotional security

5. Growth-Oriented Mindset

- ☐ I invite feedback without taking it personally
- ☐ I own my mistakes and make space for my partner's growth too
- ☐ I check in regularly to see how we're doing as a team
- ☐ I celebrate progress, not just perfection
- ☐ I view challenges as opportunities to deepen our connection

Note to Reader:

Trust is not built in grand declarations. It's built in the small, repeated choices that say: *"You matter. We matter. I'm here, and I'm not going anywhere."*

Balancing Independence and Intimacy in Relationships

"Real intimacy is not the loss of the self—it is the sharing of it. But for many of us, shaped by early attachment wounds, closeness feels risky, and distance feels safer."

In every close relationship, we are constantly managing a quiet tension: the need for autonomy and the need for connection. For securely attached individuals, this tension feels fluid—they can move in and out of closeness without fear of abandonment or engulfment.

But for those with insecure attachment styles, this balance can feel like a battleground. Intimacy may trigger fear of loss, while independence may trigger fear of rejection. Understanding this struggle is the first step toward healing it—*together*.

How Each Attachment Style Struggles with Independence vs. Intimacy

Anxious Attachment

- **Core fear:** Being unloved, left behind, or emotionally abandoned.
- **The struggle:** Closeness can feel like oxygen—and distance like danger. Anxiously attached individuals may cling when they sense their partner pulling away, unintentionally suffocating the very connection they crave.

Typical thoughts:

- "If we spend time apart, you'll forget about me."
- "Needing space means you don't love me."

Growth work: Learning that space doesn't mean rejection, and that maintaining one's identity within a relationship actually strengthens connection.

Avoidant Attachment

- **Core fear:** Losing autonomy, being engulfed, or made emotionally vulnerable.
- **The struggle:** Intimacy often triggers discomfort. Avoidantly attached individuals may pull away when emotions get too intense, interpreting closeness as a threat to their freedom.

Typical thoughts:
- "If I let you in, I'll lose myself."
- "The more you need me, the more I need to pull back."

Growth work: Learning that closeness doesn't equal control, and that emotional intimacy can be safe, reciprocal, and freely chosen.

Disorganized Attachment

- **Core fear:** Both abandonment and intimacy—often stemming from past trauma.
- **The struggle:** Intimacy is craved but feared. Individuals with disorganized attachment may vacillate unpredictably between clinginess and withdrawal, creating confusion for both themselves and their partner.

Typical thoughts:
- "I want you close, but I don't trust closeness."
- "I need you, but I'm afraid of being hurt."

Growth work: Building self-trust first, then co-creating safe, predictable interactions that support regulation and connection.

Finding Common Ground as a Couple

Couples often unconsciously polarize—one partner pursuing, the other distancing. The key is to break the cycle by:

- Naming the dynamic without blame
- Validating both needs (closeness and space)
- Creating rituals that respect both autonomy and togetherness

Examples:
- A weekly check-in to voice unmet needs without judgment
- Planned alone time *and* protected connection time
- "Connection before correction" when conflicts arise

Healthy relationships require closeness, but not at the cost of individuality. When intimacy grows, it's natural to crave emotional closeness, shared routines, and common goals. However, for a relationship to thrive over time, both partners must maintain their sense of self. Balancing independence and intimacy entails creating space for togetherness and autonomy—so that both people feel supported, not smothered; connected, not consumed.

This balance is especially important for adults navigating attachment wounds. Signs of imbalance include:

- **Too much enmeshment**: You feel responsible for your partner's emotional state, sacrifice personal goals, or find it hard to enjoy solitude without guilt.
- **Too much distance**: You avoid emotional conversations, hesitate to share your inner world, or prioritize personal space in ways that create disconnection.

Over time, either extreme can lead to resentment, confusion, or emotional erosion. The key is not choosing one over the other, but learning to move flexibly between the two.[57]

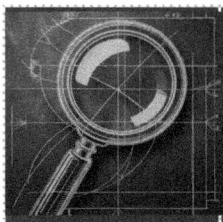

Case Glimpse: Tasha & Malik

Tasha, a rising marketing executive, began to notice tension with her partner, Malik, every time she received a promotion or traveled for work. He wasn't unsupportive, but she could feel him pulling away.

Malik, meanwhile, had grown up with a parent who was always working, physically present but emotionally absent. He didn't realize that Tasha's ambition was triggering a fear of emotional neglect.

Through couples therapy, they unpacked their attachment histories and began redefining what presence meant.

They created rituals, such as voice notes during business trips, a "no phone" dinner once a week, and regular check-ins that weren't about logistics, but about how they were doing emotionally.

Their careers didn't slow down. But neither did their connection.

Practices That Foster Balance

1. Self-Connection First
Staying connected to your own emotional world allows you to connect more authentically with your partner. Make space for solo reflection, hobbies, or quiet time. The goal is not escape, but nourishment. A grounded self brings more presence to the relationship.[58]

2. Communicate Your Needs Clearly
It's okay to need space. It's okay to need closeness. The healthiest relationships honor both. Rather than assuming your partner knows your needs, speak them aloud:

- "I'd love a quiet evening to recharge—can we plan something together tomorrow?"
- "I'm missing you lately. Can we carve out time for just us this weekend?"

When needs are expressed with clarity and care, they're more likely to be respected.

3. Mutual Support of Individual Growth

Cheer each other on in your individual pursuits—whether it's personal growth, friendships, or creative goals. When each person feels supported in becoming more fully themselves, intimacy expands.

4. Create Rituals of Togetherness

Protect moments that cultivate connection: regular check-ins, date nights, shared meals, or quiet touchpoints during busy days. These rituals help anchor the relationship, even as you pursue independent paths.

When intimacy and independence coexist, relationships feel spacious and resilient. You don't have to sacrifice closeness for freedom, or freedom for closeness. In fact, when rooted in mutual trust, the two tend to enhance one another.

Self-Discovery Exercise: "My Intimacy Map"

Use this guided journaling prompt to explore your relationship with closeness and independence.

Instructions:

Reflect on and write out your responses—no judgment, just awareness.

1. **What does intimacy feel like in my body?**
   (e.g., warm, anxious, tense, safe, overwhelming)

2. **When someone gets emotionally close to me, I tend to...**
   (e.g., open up, panic, shut down, cling, test them)

3. **When I need space, I feel...**
   (e.g., guilty, relieved, disconnected, selfish, secure)

4. **What I wish my partner understood about how I experience closeness is...**

5. **What helps me feel connected without losing myself is...**

Have your partner complete it too, then exchange and discuss your maps.

Understanding Love Languages: Enhancing Connection

Love is often described as feelings, but it's more accurately how you express those feelings and how you receive them. Partners can deeply care for one another and still feel disconnected if their ways of giving and receiving love don't align. This is where the concept of love languages becomes a powerful tool.

Popularized by Dr. Gary Chapman, the idea of love languages refers to five primary ways people express and experience emotional affection: Words of Affirmation, Acts of Service, Receiving Gifts, Quality Time, and Physical Touch.[59] Understanding these languages helps partners translate care in a way that resonates emotionally.

The Five Love Languages

1. Words of Affirmation
Verbal expressions of love, appreciation, and encouragement. Phrases like *"I'm proud of you"* or *"You mean so much to me"* strengthen emotional security.

2. Acts of Service
Actions over words. Helping with daily responsibilities, running errands, or making a thoughtful gesture communicates love through support and reliability.

3. Receiving Gifts
It's not about materialism—it's about symbolic meaning. A small, thoughtful token says, *"I was thinking of you."*

4. Quality Time

Focused attention and shared experiences—uninterrupted and intentional—create connection. This might look like deep conversation, shared hobbies, or simply being present.

5. Physical Touch

Affectionate physical contact, such as holding hands, hugging, or sitting close, provides reassurance and intimacy.

Each person typically has one or two primary languages that make them feel most loved. Misalignment can lead to unintentional hurt: one partner may consistently express love, but the other may not feel it.

Discovering Your Love Language(s)

Use the tool provided below, or you can also take a short assessment developed by Chapman to clarify your preferences.[60]

"Love is not just a feeling—it's a language.
To feel fully connected, we must learn to speak and hear
it in ways that resonate with the hearts involved."

Self-Discovery Exercise: "My Intimacy Map"

A self-awareness tool to explore your unique patterns of connection.

Instructions

For each of the following 20 statements, rate how true it fels for you **on a scale from 1 to 5**:

1 = Not true at all

3 = Somewhat true

5 = Very true

You'll rate both **how you give love** and **how you like to receive love** to see if they match—or differ.

Part One: How I Prefer to RECEIVE Love

1. I feel most connected when someone gives me their full attention—no phones, no distractions.
2. Being hugged, kissed, or gently touched helps me feel emotionally grounded.
3. When someone helps me with a task (even small ones), I feel deeply cared for.
4. Hearing "I love you" or other verbal affirmations makes me feel secure.
5. I light up when I receive thoughtful gifts or surprises—it shows me I was remembered.
6. When someone listens to my worries without jumping in to fix them, I feel truly loved.
7. Small physical gestures (like a hand on my back or sitting close) mean a lot to me.
8. When my partner handles a responsibility without me asking, it builds trust.
9. Compliments and loving words lift my mood quickly.
10. I keep and cherish little things people give me—cards, notes, gifts—because they remind me I matter.

Part Two: How I Tend to GIVE Love

11. I'm intentional about setting aside time to be fully present with the people I love.
12. I show love through physical affection—hugs, touch, leaning in.
13. I often do practical things—errands, chores, problem-solving—as a way to care for others.
14. I express love through compliments, encouragement, or saying "I'm proud of you."
15. I enjoy picking out or making meaningful gifts for others.
16. I prefer deep, uninterrupted conversation over small talk.
17. I naturally reach out to hold hands, sit close, or offer hugs.
18. I anticipate others' needs and try to take care of things before being asked.
19. I often leave little notes, send affirming texts, or say "I love you" throughout the day.
20. I get joy from surprising people I love with thoughtful tokens or plans.

SCORING GUIDE

Group your responses by Love Language category. Add up the total for **Part One (Receiving)** and **Part Two (Giving)** separately.

Love Language	Questions (Receiving)	Questions (Giving)
Quality Time	1, 6, 16	11, 16
Physical Touch	2, 7, 17	12, 17
Acts of Service	3, 8, 18	13, 18
Words of Affirmation	4, 9, 19	14, 19
Gift Giving	5, 10, 20	15, 20

Step 1: Total your scores for each language in both sections.

Step 2: Compare: Are your preferred ways of receiving love the same as how you naturally give love?

Interpreting Your Results

Matching Styles: You give and receive love in the same way. This often feels intuitive and satisfying in relationships—*but only if your partner shares the same preferences.*

Differing Styles: Many people express love one way and receive it another. For example, you may give love through acts of service but long to receive verbal affirmation. This can lead to mismatches in relationships if not communicated clearly.

Why This Matters (Attachment Perspective)

Anxious attachers may prioritize **words of affirmation** or **quality time**—reassurance and presence soothe fear of disconnection.

Avoidant attachers often express love through **acts of service** or **gifting**, which feel "safe" and less vulnerable than direct emotional closeness.

Disorganized attachers may swing between extremes—clinging to verbal or physical expressions one moment, withdrawing the next. Their love language may be less about preference and more about **feeling safe enough to receive**.

Reflection Prompts

1. What surprised you about your top love language for giving and receiving?
2. Is there a mismatch between how you give and what you most need?
3. In your closest relationship, how do you think your partner prefers to receive love?
4. What's one small way you can try speaking their love language this week?

**BONUS:
Partner Conversation Starter**

"I learned something about how I give and receive love. Would you be open to exploring this with me? I think it could help us understand each other better."

Practicing Love Languages in Relationships

1. Have the Conversation
Talk about your love languages with your partner. Share examples of what makes you feel most connected.

2. Respect the Difference
You don't have to share the same love language, but learning your partner's is an act of care in itself. Loving someone in the way they best receive it is a choice you make, again and again.

3. Integrate Love Languages Into Daily Life
Try small, consistent acts. Leave a note (Words of Affirmation), offer to make coffee (Acts of Service), plan a distraction-free hour together (Quality Time), give a long hug (Physical Touch), or surprise them with their favorite treat (Receiving Gifts).

When love is spoken fluently in both directions, relationships deepen. Understanding love languages tunes you into what helps you and your partner feel safe, valued, and emotionally seen.

Navigating Conflict: Turning Challenges into Opportunities

Conflict is not a sign that something is broken—it's a sign that something needs attention. Every relationship, no matter how secure or loving, experiences moments of friction. What matters most is how those moments are handled. When approached mindfully, conflict can become a gateway to deeper understanding, emotional growth, and renewed trust.

Unresolved conflict, however, can create emotional distance. Silence, blame, and avoidance often feel safer than saying the hard thing. But over time, this avoidance erodes connection. The goal isn't to eliminate conflict altogether, but learn how to navigate it compassionately and respectfully.[62]

Why Conflict Feels So Threatening

Conflict often activates our nervous system's threat response. Raised voices, criticism, or withdrawal can trigger old wounds and attachment fears. This is especially true for individuals with anxious or avoidant patterns, who may interpret disagreement as rejection or emotional danger.[51]

The first step in navigating conflict skillfully is recognizing your default response—fight, flight, freeze, or fawn—and learning how to regulate your emotions before engaging.

Handled well, conflict allows partners to:

- Clarify misunderstood needs or values
- Express vulnerability that strengthens intimacy
- Repair emotional ruptures and build resilience
- Learn how each person copes under stress

When both people stay engaged, even in discomfort, conflict becomes less of a threat and more of a turning point.

Techniques for Navigating Conflict

1. Use a Softened Start-Up
How you begin matters. Instead of launching with blame ("You never listen to me"), try a gentle opening that centers your own experience:

> "I've been feeling a bit distant lately, and I'd like us to reconnect."

Softened start-ups reduce defensiveness and keep both partners more regulated.[57]

2. Slow Down Reactivity
If you feel emotionally flooded—tight chest, racing heart, mental fog—pause. Take a break, regulate your nervous system, and return when you're calmer. Say:

> "I care about this conversation. I just need a little space to collect my thoughts."

This prevents escalation and supports productive dialogue.

3. Stay on the Topic
Avoid bringing up unrelated past grievances. Stick to one issue at a time. Ask:

> "What are we really trying to resolve here?"

This helps keep the conversation focused and less emotionally overwhelming.

4. Validate, Even When You Disagree
You don't have to agree to validate your partner's feelings. Try:
> "I can see why that felt hurtful to you."

Validation communicates emotional safety and encourages openness.

5. Commit to Repair

Conflict resolution doesn't require a perfect outcome—it requires a willingness to repair. This may mean offering a sincere apology, clarifying misunderstandings, or simply saying:

> "I see where I missed you. Thank you for helping me understand."

All relationships face rupture. The most resilient ones know how to repair. When conflict becomes a conversation, not a battleground, it creates space for connection—even in the hardest moments.

Scene: "The Look"— A Moment of Repair

The Couple:

Jonah (42, he/him): Quiet, introspective, formerly emotionally unavailable. Had a brief affair three years ago. Since then, has been doing deep self-work—therapy, accountability, presence.

Camille (39, she/her): Warm, intuitive, historically over-functioned in the relationship. Still healing the part of her that scans for betrayal even when things are going well.

They've been doing better. Stronger. More connected. But some moments still carry echoes.

It happened at a dinner party.

One of Jonah's coworkers—a woman Camille had never met—laughed a little too long at his story. Camille noticed the way Jonah smiled back. The flicker of shared energy. It lasted only a second, but her body remembered everything.

On the drive home, the silence was thick.

Finally, Jonah asked, "You're quiet. Everything okay?"

Camille didn't want to ruin the night. But she knew that swallowing her discomfort would only feed the fear. So she exhaled.

> "There was a moment… when you were talking to your coworker. The way you laughed with her—it reminded me of before. My stomach dropped. I know it was probably nothing. But my body still panicked."

Jonah felt the air shift. The old guilt surfaced. But he caught himself. He didn't say, *"It wasn't a big deal,"* or *"You're overreacting."* He didn't get defensive.

He turned toward her in the passenger seat and said, softly:

> "Thank you for telling me. I know that must have been hard to say. And I hate that I gave you a reason in the past to feel that way."

Camille nodded, eyes glassy.

> "I didn't want to accuse you. I just needed you to know what came up for me."

Jonah reached for her hand.

> "I see that. And I want you to know—there was nothing flirtatious about that moment. But your feelings are real. And I want to be the kind of partner who makes you feel secure, not scared."

She squeezed his hand. Her chest softened.

> "That helps more than you know."

The car kept moving forward. And so did they.

Narrative Insight: What Repair Looks Like

Repair doesn't mean the pain never resurfaces. It means there's space to talk about it without shame or shutdown. In this moment, Camille stayed in her vulnerability, and Jonah stayed present in his responsibility.

The past didn't swallow them. They walked through it—together.

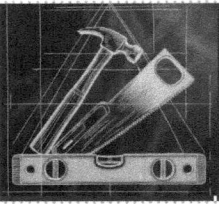

Conflict De-escalation Script

For use during heated or emotionally overwhelming moments. This script helps couples pause, reset, and re-enter a conflict with more emotional regulation and clarity.

Step 1: Pause & Acknowledge

Each partner uses language that avoids blame and affirms the value of the relationship.

"I can feel myself getting overwhelmed. I care about you and this conversation, so I'd like to take a short break to calm down."

"This matters to me. I want to stay respectful, so I need a moment to breathe."

Step 2: Regulate & Reflect (Take 10-30 Minutes Apart)

Use this time to regulate your nervous system:

- Deep breathing
- Grounding (feet on the floor, focus on breath)
- Journaling what you're feeling
- Going for a short walk

Ask yourself:

- What am I feeling?
- What do I need right now (clarity, comfort, space)?
- What is the core issue beneath my reaction?

Step 3: Reconnect & Reset the Tone

Return and take turns sharing calmly. Use this language:
- "Thanks for giving us both space to reflect. I'm ready to talk with care."
- "I've had a chance to think, and I want to understand what you're feeling."
- Use "I feel" statements and stay curious. End with:
- "I still care deeply about how we move through this—together."

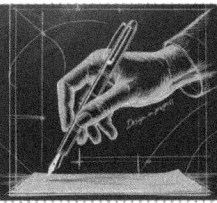

Repair Reflection Page: Rebuilding After Conflict or Disconnection

Every relationship has ruptures. What matters most is how we return to each other afterward.

Step 1: What Happened?

Describe the situation or moment of disconnection. (Try to stick to the facts—what was said or done.)

What emotions did you feel during or after the conflict?

☐ Hurt

☐ Anger

☐ Sadness

☐ Shame

☐ Frustration

☐ Disappointment

☐ Confusion

☐ Fear

☐ Other:

Step 2: What Was Underneath the Reaction?

What core need might have gone unmet in that moment?

☐ To feel heard

☐ To feel respected

☐ To feel safe

☐ To feel loved

☐ To feel valued

☐ To feel supported

Other:

What story did your mind start telling you?

(e.g., "They don't care," "I always mess this up," "They never listen to me.")

Step 3: Express What You Wish You'd Said (or Still Want to Say)

Use this sentence starter to bring repair through vulnerability:

"What I really needed in that moment was _____. I felt _____, and I wish I had said _____."

Step 4: What Do You Want to Offer or Ask For?

Choose or write your own repair intention:

☐ I want to offer a sincere apology

☐ I want to ask for reassurance or clarity

☐ I want to reconnect emotionally

☐ I want to create a healthier way to handle similar moments

☐ I want to listen more fully next time

Other:

What would help you or your partner feel safe moving forward?

Step 5: Reflect on the Experience

1. What did this moment teach you about your relationship dynamic?
2. What can I do to take responsibility for my part in the conflict?
3. What do I want to say to repair this rupture?
4. What boundary or change might help us handle this differently next time?
5. What do you want to remember the next time things feel tense or disconnected?

Reminder: Repair isn't about erasing the rupture. It's about showing your partner that the connection matters more than the conflict.

Repair Ritual Guide

Rebuilding safety and connection after conflict

A ritualized, shared practice for couples to engage in after emotionally charged moments. This can be used post-conflict—even if the disagreement isn't fully resolved yet.

Step 1: Physical Reconnection

Sit together without speaking. Make eye contact, hold hands, or sit with knees touching for one minute. Breathe together.

This silent reconnection reminds the body that your partner is not a threat.

Step 2: Acknowledge and Affirm

Each partner takes a turn completing these prompts:

- "What I wish I had done differently was…"
- "What I appreciate about you—even in the hard moments—is…"
- "One way I want to show up better next time is…"

Step 3: Offer & Receive Repair

This might include:

- A sincere apology
- A moment of shared humor or affection
- A phrase of reassurance (e.g., "We're still on the same team")

Optional Closing Ritual

Choose one of the following to end:

- 3 deep breaths together
- A warm hug or hand on the heart
- Say: "We can do hard things—together."

Avoiding Common Relationship Pitfalls: Lessons Learned

Even the most loving relationships can develop patterns that gradually erode connection. These patterns rarely emerge overnight. They accumulate in small, often unnoticed ways: miscommunication, unmet needs, unspoken resentment, and emotional avoidance. What is the good news? With awareness and intention, the majority of these pitfalls can be identified and corrected before they cause major damage.

As we conclude this chapter on cultivating healthy relationships, it's worth pausing to consider some of the most common mistakes couples make—and the lessons we can learn from them.

1. Mistaking Closeness for Clarity

Spending time together doesn't guarantee emotional understanding. Many couples assume their partner *should know* what they're feeling or needing—especially after years together. But assumptions breed disappointment, and longevity almost always means change. Even if you did know what your partner needed for several years, what your partner needs today might be different. One of the most important relational habits is to express needs clearly and without blame, even when it feels vulnerable.[53]

> **Lesson:** Don't confuse proximity with connection. Say what you mean. Ask what they need. Keep the channel open.

2. Avoiding Conflict to "Keep the Peace"

Conflict avoidance may seem like a shortcut to harmony, but it often creates long-term disconnection. Over time, unspoken frustrations build into emotional walls. Small issues become symbolic of larger wounds, and intimacy suffers.

Lesson: Disagreement is not a threat, but an opportunity. Lean into repair, not retreat.

3. Losing Yourself in the Relationship
In the name of closeness, it's easy to abandon personal interests, routines, or friendships. But without a separate sense of self, resentment often grows. A healthy relationship supports individuality and togetherness in equal measure.[57]

Lesson: Nurture your own life, so you can show up to the relationship with energy and authenticity.

4. Using Protection Instead of Presence
When emotional safety feels uncertain, people often protect themselves with defensiveness, sarcasm, withdrawal, or control. These strategies may feel safer in the moment, but block the vulnerability required for true intimacy.[51]

Lesson: The antidote to emotional armor is emotional honesty. Risk being seen.

5. Expecting Change Without Communication
Hoping your partner will change through hints, silence, or disappointment rarely works. Growth comes from curiosity, dialogue, and mutual commitment—not pressure or resentment.

Lesson: Invite change through compassion, not control.

Healthy relationships are not the result of avoiding difficulty. They grow stronger through the willingness to navigate it with kindness, courage, and humility. If you've recognized any of these patterns in your own relationship, take heart: noticing is the first step toward healing.

Every conversation, repair, and shared moment of honesty builds a stronger and more resilient connection. Relationships do not need to be perfect to be beautiful. They just need to be practiced together.

Checklist: New Patterns for Positive Interactions

Simple habits that build emotional safety, connection, and relational trust.

Daily Communication Rituals

☐ Greet your partner warmly each morning ("Good morning, I'm glad you're here")

☐ Say goodbye with intention—even if it's just a 10-second hug

☐ Check in once during the day (text or voice note) to say, "Thinking of you"

☐ Share one thing you appreciate about them—out loud or in writing

☐ End the day with a brief "What went well today?" conversation or cuddle

Connection Over Correction

☐ Start hard conversations with *"Can we talk about something?"* instead of launching into a complaint

☐ Pause before reacting—breathe, then respond with curiosity

☐ Practice "I feel..." statements instead of "You always..." or "You never..."

☐ Soften your face and tone when discussing something difficult

☐ Acknowledge your part in conflict—even if it's just tone or timing

Rituals That Rewire

☐ Create a weekly "connection check-in" (10–15 min of open sharing)

☐ Revisit a shared happy memory together (photos, playlists, stories)

☐ Make a "Just Because" gesture—coffee, a note, a kind message

☐ Use a shared word or phrase as a signal for needing closeness (e.g., "bridge time")

☐ Designate device-free time each day (start small—5 minutes counts)

Emotional Support on Purpose

☐ Ask: *"How can I support you right now?"* (instead of assuming)

☐ Say: *"I'm here for you. I don't have to fix it—I just want to stay close."*

☐ Practice small, safe touch—hand on back, gentle squeeze, eye contact

☐ Celebrate small wins or progress ("I saw how hard you tried today")

☐ Validate feelings, even if you don't share the same reaction

Relational Growth Habits

☐ Set shared intentions (e.g., "Let's try speaking gently even when tired")

☐ Ask once a week: *"How are we doing—anything we could do differently?"*

☐ Read or listen to a relationship resource together and discuss

☐ Try a new experience together—novelty builds trust and joy

☐ Say "thank you" more often, especially for the *little things*

Reminder: You don't have to do all of these at once. Choose 1–2 to begin practicing consistently. Small shifts, done with care, create big emotional rewiring over time.

04

Enhancing Family Bonds

We sat together in my brother's condo that quiet afternoon, sunlight angling through the windows like it could cast light on our hidden truths. I shared my vision—carefully, honestly—for what I wanted our marriage to become.

Paul and I named the kind of love we each longed for, the kind of partnership we hoped we could still co-create. I offered specific examples of behaviors I needed from someone who respected me—small, tangible ways to show up with care and intention. He asked clarifying questions to make sure he understood. We even spoke the bigger dreams aloud: the ones we used to share. The life I still hoped we might build together, if we could learn to meet each other differently.

Paul remained calm and open, more present than I'd seen him in years. It felt like a rare and protective bubble had formed around us, holding our raw, open-hearted selves in a space neither of us had been brave enough to create before. In that moment, we weren't adversaries. We were two people trying to find our way back to each other.

From the guest room, our son stirred.

> *"It's going to take work," I said softly, glancing toward the door, "but I'm willing to try if you are. He deserves to see his parents happy and healthy. He deserves to know what love looks like."*

Paul nodded and rose to retrieve our baby, returning with a quiet smile and a bundle in his arms. I watched the two of them, father and son, and felt a swell of something more profound than resolve. This little person was where my courage came from.

Looking at our son, I saw all the fragile hope I had once carried as a child: the desperate wish to be held in safe, enduring love. He had no reason to inherit anything less. And he certainly didn't deserve to.

Paul and I had both come from divorced families and complex, blended households. There had been love, yes, but also rupture. There was protection, but also absence. We grew up in environments where emotional survival sometimes looked like silence, or shutting down, or shouldering more than a child ever should.

Our parents did the best they could with the tools they had. But we had access to more. And if there was even a chance to do better, to model something different for the next generation, I wanted to take it.

We agreed to take the next week apart as a gentle pause—a chance to reflect, to reset, and to begin imagining a different way forward. One rooted in growth.

What I didn't fully understand then is that becoming a parent had changed me in ways I couldn't yet articulate. It had rewired my brain, restructured my values, and reawakened something ancient and fierce in me: a longing to protect not just my child's body, but his emotional world.

And to do that, I had to begin tending to my own.

Parenting changes you—practically, neurologically, relationally, emotionally. It peels back layers you didn't know were there. It magnifies the emotional blueprints you inherited. And for many of us, it becomes the great mirror: one that shows us how we love, how we communicate, how we react when we're overwhelmed.

It also shows us what we want to change.

In the next chapter, we'll look at how attachment manifests in family systems, including between parents and children, siblings and carers, and across generations and cultures. We'll explore how to model secure relationships for the children watching us. How to co-create emotionally safe homes. How to make space for the parts of our children and ourselves that have never learned to feel safe expressing our needs.

Because the truth is, healing does not stop with us. It flows through us—into the families we're raising, the homes we're shaping, and the love we choose to give.

Addressing Attachment Styles in Family Dynamics

> *"Attachment doesn't stop at romance. It's a blueprint that lives in the kitchen, the group chat, the holidays, and the unspoken rules of closeness and distance."*

Family is often the original arena where our attachment patterns take shape and then continue to play out. Whether we're dealing with aging parents, grown siblings, or our own children, the way we relate, repair, and retreat within our family system is often shaped by the attachment strategies we learned early in life.

Let's explore how each style might
show up in everyday family life:

1. Secure Attachment: "I can be close and still be me."
People with secure attachment are generally able to stay connected to family members without losing themselves. They can offer support without feeling burdened, set boundaries without guilt, and repair conflict without spiraling into shame or blame.

Example:

Michelle, a securely attached adult daughter, gets critical comments from her mother about her parenting style. Instead of shutting down or attacking, Michelle says,

> "I know you want the best for the kids, but that comment didn't land well. Can we talk about it?"

She holds her boundary *and* her connection.

Secure hallmarks in families:

- Can tolerate differences without losing closeness
- Reaches out during hard times, but doesn't demand rescue
- Resolves conflict through repair and reflection, not retaliation

2. Anxious Attachment: "If we're not close, something must be wrong."
Anxiously attached individuals often seek constant emotional reassurance in their family relationships. They may feel responsible for everyone's emotional state and fear being excluded, forgotten, or unloved. In the absence of emotional closeness, they may interpret distance as rejection.

Example:

Max is the youngest sibling in a large family. When his older siblings make plans without including him, he doesn't ask about it directly. Instead, he texts vague comments like,

> "Guess I didn't make the cut again 🙃"

He's not trying to guilt-trip—he's trying to feel seen—but his communication style may push others away.

Anxious hallmarks in families:

- Over-texting, over-apologizing, or over-giving to maintain connection
- Reads into tone, timing, or silence
- May fear setting boundaries in case they threaten belonging

3. Avoidant Attachment: "I'm fine—just don't ask me to need anyone." Avoidantly attached individuals may appear independent, but beneath the surface, they often harbor a deep-seated fear that relying on others will lead to disappointment or loss of control. In family settings, this can manifest as emotional distance, a tendency to avoid deep conversations, or withdrawal during conflicts.

Example:

Leah rarely answers family group texts. When she visits her parents, she offers to fix the sink or run errands, but won't sit down to talk about feelings. If a sibling brings up childhood trauma, Leah changes the subject or says,

> "I don't see the point in rehashing the past."

Avoidant hallmarks in families:

- Shows love through actions, not words
- Keeps emotions tightly guarded
- Disengages during emotional moments, even if unintentionally

4. Disorganized Attachment: "I want closeness, but it doesn't feel safe."

Disorganized attachment is often rooted in early relational trauma—where the caregiver was both a source of love and fear. These individuals may crave closeness in family relationships but feel overwhelmed, mistrustful, or reactive when they get it. Their responses may appear inconsistent or confusing to others.

Example:

Jules, who experienced childhood neglect, goes home for Thanksgiving. At first, she's bubbly and affectionate. After her dad makes a minor comment about her career, she shuts down, lashes out, and leaves early. Later, she texts her sister:

> "I don't know why I even try. They always make me feel like garbage."

Disorganized hallmarks in families:

- Intense highs and lows in closeness
- Distrust of others' intentions, even in loving gestures
- May push others away and feel hurt when they stay away

Family systems are often the *origin* of our attachment patterns and, when approached with awareness and compassion, they can also be the space where we begin to rewire them.

"Healing doesn't mean never getting triggered—it means learning how to reconnect without self-abandonment or blame."

By recognizing and wholeheartedly embracing the diverse attachment styles inhabiting your family, you create a sanctuary of growth and acceptance. Your home expands beyond a residence to a refuge—a nurturing space where every member is affirmed, supported, and equipped to face the world's complexities in love and unity.

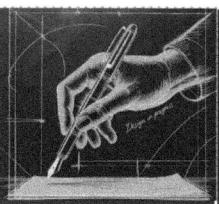

Journal Prompt: Reflecting on Your Role in the Family Emotional System

"Family patterns are often passed down unconsciously—until someone chooses to see them clearly and respond with intention instead of instinct."

Use this prompt to explore your place in your family's emotional landscape:

Prompt:

1. What emotional role did I learn to play in my family growing up? (e.g., peacekeeper, fixer, rebel, emotional sponge, go-between)

2. How do I typically respond when a family member gets upset? Do I feel responsible, overwhelmed, indifferent, or activated?

3. When I speak up in my family, do I feel heard—or hesitant? Why?

4. What's one pattern I want to unlearn—and one I want to build?

5. What kind of family member do I want to *become* moving forward?

Family Communication Activity: "Mapping Our Patterns"

A collaborative activity to bring awareness to the way your family communicates and connects. Gently explore recurring emotional roles and interaction patterns in the family, identify what's working, and spark conversations around trust, safety, and change.

Step 1: Reflect (Solo or Together)

Use the prompts below to reflect individually. If doing this as a family, each member should answer for themselves first.

1. **When conflict arises in our family, I tend to...**
   ☐ Speak up quickly
   ☐ Shut down or withdraw
   ☐ Try to fix everything
   ☐ Avoid the topic
   ☐ Make jokes or change the subject
   ☐ Something else:

2. **When I feel hurt in our family, I usually...**
   ☐ Say something directly
   ☐ Keep it to myself
   ☐ Distance myself emotionally or physically
   ☐ Let it build up and then explode
   ☐ Try to forgive quickly without talking about it

3. **One thing I wish was easier to say in our family is...**

4. **When I feel most connected to my family, it's because...**

Step 2: Share and Discuss (If Safe & Willing)

Create a low-pressure space to share responses. Choose one or two questions to discuss at a time. Listen and get curious about how different family members experience the same space.

Use reflective listening tools:

"What I'm hearing is…"

"That makes sense because…"

"Thank you for sharing that with me."

Optional: Create a New Pattern Together

Choose *one* new practice you'd like to try as a family:

☐ Weekly family check-in

☐ "Pause and breathe" rule in arguments

☐ Family affirmation jar (each person adds kind notes)

☐ Clear-out time for unresolved feelings

☐ Setting boundaries around gossip, sarcasm, or rehashing old conflicts

Write it down:

"We are going to try _____ for the next week as a new way of showing up for each other."

**BONUS:
Family Conversation Starter**

"I read something recently that made me think about how we all learned to deal with emotions differently—based on what we saw and needed growing up. Would you be open to talking sometime about what helped or hurt, and how we could do things differently going forward—especially when we hit tough moments?"

Conscious Parenting: Understanding Your Emotional Influence

Children learn more from what you model than what you instruct. They observe not just what you say, but how you say it, how you handle frustration, how you show affection, and how you repair after rupture. These everyday behaviors create the emotional blueprint your child will carry into their own relationships.[7]

Conscious parenting—as with emotional intelligence and effective communication—begins with self-awareness. It means recognizing how your moods, stress responses, and coping strategies shape your child's sense of safety. When you respond with patience rather than reactivity—even imperfectly—you teach resilience. When you name your emotions and model regulation, you offer them a roadmap for handling their own inner world.[64]

Children don't need flawless caregivers. They need caregivers who are honest, responsive, and emotionally available. When you show them it's okay to apologize, take a break, or revisit a conversation with more clarity, you teach them flexibility, humility, and repair.

Practices for Conscious Parenting

- Reflect daily: *What emotional tone did I set today? How did I respond to stress?*
- Narrate emotional experiences: "I'm feeling frustrated right now, so I'm taking a few breaths."
- Pause before reacting. Ask: *Is my response helpful, or just habitual?*
- Prioritize connection over correction. Especially during emotional moments, attunement is more important than a solution.

By tending to your own emotional state, you become a more stable anchor for your child. You teach them, without words, how to become one for themselves.

Creating Emotionally Safe Homes: Modeling Secure Attachments in Everyday Life

A secure home still has conflicts, but is rich in repair. It's a space where emotions are allowed, voices are heard, and mistakes are met with care. In this kind of environment, children grow up knowing *I am safe. I am seen. I can be imperfect and still be loved.*

Secure attachment is built through consistency, attunement, and responsiveness. You don't have to solve every problem on demand. Instead, be present and follow through when you say you will. Create predictable, regular rituals of care, like shared meals, bedtime check-ins, or simply putting down your phone when your child speaks.[65]

Case Study: "The Drawing"— How Everyday Moments Shape Attachment

Small, often unconscious parenting moments shape a child's internal working model of attachment. This story illustrates how parental presence and emotional attunement can either unintentionally reinforce insecurity or build the foundation for a secure connection.

The Setup:

Emma is a 6-year-old girl. Her mother, Julia, is a loving but chronically busy parent, juggling a demanding job, household responsibilities, and an endless to-do list. Emma comes home from school one afternoon, clutching a drawing she made of the two of them. It's simple—just crayon lines and a big red heart—but to Emma, it means something. She's trying to connect.

Version 1: Missed Moment—Anxious Internalization

Julia is typing furiously on her laptop at the dining room table. The laundry buzzes. Her phone pings with a Slack notification. She's on her third cup of coffee.

Emma walks in, hopeful.

> "Mommy, look! I made this for you!"

Julia glances up, smiles quickly, and says,

> "Oh, that's nice, sweetie. Put it on the counter, okay? I've got to finish something."

Emma's face falls, but she nods. She places the drawing on the cluttered counter, next to the unopened mail and grocery receipts. She lingers for a moment, hoping for more. Julia doesn't look up again.

Emma walks away quietly.

What the child learns (unconsciously):
- *My excitement can be inconvenient.*
- *When I try to connect, I might be dismissed.*
- *To get love, I need to earn it by not requiring too much.*

Later, Julia will tuck Emma into bed and say, "I love you." And she *does*. But a part of Emma's nervous system has already logged the moment: Connection is uncertain. My needs might be too much.

This is how an anxious or avoidant attachment template begins—not through trauma, but through repetition of micro-moments where emotional bids are missed.

Version 2: Attuned Response—Secure Internalization

Julia is still typing at the table. The house hums with busyness. But when Emma walks in with her drawing, Julia notices the hopeful look on her daughter's face—the way she clutches the paper like a treasure.

She pauses.

"Whoa... did you make that for me?"

Emma nods, her eyes wide.

Julia closes the laptop halfway and turns toward her daughter.

"Tell me about it—what's happening here?"

Emma points out the heart.

"That's us. I made it during free time. I wanted to make something about love."

Julia places her hand over her heart.

"You really know how to make someone feel special. Can I hang this on the fridge now—or would you like to help me pick the perfect spot?"

Emma beams. Her body softens. Her need to connect is met. She skips away singing.

What the child learns (unconsciously):
- *My feelings matter to the people I love.*
- *When I reach out, someone will meet me there.*
- *It's safe to express love—and to receive it.*

Later, Julia returns to work. But the emotional message has landed: Love is not something I have to earn. It's something I can trust.

Narrative Insight: Why This Moment Matters

When it comes to parenting, remember it's all about presence over perfection. You don't have to nail it every time. In fact, I promise that you won't. And yet secure attachment can and does still flourish because even short moments of attunement can rewire the attachment system, helping children internalize the most secure message of all:

> "When I show you who I am and what I need, you don't turn away. You turn toward."

The long-term benefits of cultivating an emotionally supportive home are profound. As emotional support becomes ingrained in family life, stress and conflict naturally diminish. Families who prioritize emotional safety often find that their relationships improve, with members showing increased resilience during life's challenges. Children raised in such environments grow up with a stronger sense of self-worth, equipped to form healthy relationships beyond the family unit.

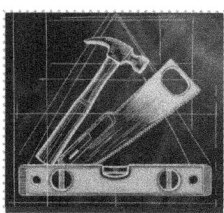

Checklist: Responding to Your Child's Emotional Bids

Tiny, everyday habits to help children feel seen, safe, and securely connected.

Step 1: Recognize the Emotional Bid

- ☐ Children don't always say, *"I need connection."* Instead, they signal it in a thousand tiny ways. Look for:
- ☐ Sudden bursts of sharing ("Look what I made!" or "Guess what happened today!")
- ☐ Seeking physical closeness (crawling onto your lap, touching your arm)
- ☐ Silly or disruptive behavior (sometimes a bid for attention or co-regulation)
- ☐ Repeating the same question or story (a cue they want more engagement)
- ☐ Quiet hovering or lingering nearby (waiting for an invitation to connect)

Ask yourself: "Is this a behavior to manage—or a connection to make?"

Step 2: Turn Toward Instead of Away

Even a small turn toward your child's emotional bid can rewire trust. Try:

- ☐ Make eye contact or gently place a hand on them
- ☐ Use warmth in your tone ("Tell me more about that!")
- ☐ Mirror their excitement or curiosity
- ☐ Pause your task briefly—even for 30 seconds—to give full presence
- ☐ If you *can't* connect in the moment, name it and commit to a time:

"I want to hear about that. Let me finish this in 10 minutes so I can really listen."

Step 3: Build Consistent Repair Routines

- ☐ Apologize sincerely if you miss a cue: e.g. "I didn't realize you were trying to share something important. I'm sorry I brushed it off."
- ☐ Make amends with presence, not just words
- ☐ Reflect together: "When you're excited or upset, what helps you feel heard by me?"
- ☐ Build rituals of connection: bedtime check-ins, daily hugs, drawing time, etc.

Bonus: Practices that Cultivate a Secure Base

- ☐ Share your own small feelings out loud to model emotional literacy
- ☐ Use "I noticed" statements: e.g. "I noticed you looked sad when I was on my phone. I'm here now."
- ☐ Avoid shaming when your child expresses big feelings
- ☐ Celebrate emotional openness, not just achievements
- ☐ Make time for one-on-one connection—even 10 minutes counts

While we always want to be on the proactive side of the equation, the reality is we can often find ourselves attempting to recreate an emotionally safe environment after we've made a mistake. Just as with any relationship, perfection isn't the expectation. Yes, even when you are the parent. You will lose your temper, feel overwhelmed, and do and say things that you wish you hadn't.

Repair is what matters.

Practicing proper repair in front of and with your children is just as important–if not more so–in building that emotionally supportive environment. Repair and reconnection models help your children metaphorically get back up after stumbling over their words and intentions. It shows them that they don't have to be perfect; they can always make things better if they are willing.

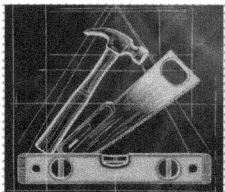

Parent-Child Repair Scripts

For when you've said or done something hurtful—and want to make it right.

1. After Yelling or Losing Patience

"I raised my voice earlier, and I could see it scared or hurt you. I'm really sorry. You didn't deserve that. I was feeling overwhelmed, but it's not okay to take that out on you. You're important to me, and I want you to feel safe with me—even when I'm having a hard moment."

2. After Ignoring or Dismissing Their Feelings

"Earlier, when you were trying to tell me how you felt, I didn't listen the way I should have. I rushed past your feelings, and I'm sorry. Your emotions matter, and I want you to know you can always come to me—even when I don't respond perfectly."

3. After Saying Something Shaming or Critical

"I said something that wasn't kind, and I regret it. My words came from frustration, not truth. You are not too much. You are not bad. You are learning and growing, and so am I. I love you exactly as you are."

4. After Failing to Show Up or Breaking a Promise

"I didn't keep my promise to you today, and I know that hurt. I let you down. You were counting on me, and I want you to know that your trust matters to me. I'll work hard to show you that I mean what I say."

5. When Reconnecting After Emotional Distance

"I know I've felt far away lately—and I imagine that might feel confusing or lonely. That distance wasn't about you. Sometimes grown-ups have big feelings too, and I'm learning how to handle them better. But I want to reconnect with you. I miss our closeness."

6. When You Don't Know Exactly What to Say, But Want to Begin

"I know I messed up, and I want to make things right. I may not have all the right words, but I care about how you feel. Can we talk about it? I want to hear what it was like for you."

Tips for Repairing with Your Child

- Use a calm tone and gentle body language
- Avoid blaming or justifying your behavior
- Focus on the impact, not just the intention
- Offer hugs or touch (if welcomed)
- Follow up with changed behavior

Reminder: Repair teaches your child that love is resilient, mistakes are survivable, and emotional safety is always worth returning to.

Children internalize these moments. When they witness empathy, they mirror it. When they experience emotional regulation, they learn to regulate. When they see you handle conflict with compassion, they feel safe expressing themselves.

Habits That Model Secure Attachment

- **Name and validate emotions**—yours and theirs. "It makes sense you're upset right now. I'm here with you."
- **Repair quickly and sincerely.** A simple: "I was impatient earlier, and I'm sorry. Let's try again," goes a long way.
- **Support autonomy.** Let them try, fail, and return to your support. Independence grows when children know they have a secure base to come back to.[1]

Invite open dialogue. Ask, "What was the best and hardest part of your day?" and really listen.

Over time, these habits create a felt sense of emotional safety that follows children into adulthood. They become more resilient, more compassionate, and more capable of forming healthy bonds.

By weaving these practices into daily life, families can cultivate an environment where everyone feels valued and understood. In such homes, love transforms from an ideal to a lived experience, providing the foundation for deeper bonds and resilience against life's tempests.

Secure attachment is created in thousands of micro-moments, far more so than grand gestures. Through your tone, your presence, your follow-through, and your capacity for repair, you lay the foundation for your child's lifelong relational health.

Creating an emotionally safe space transforms your home into more than just four walls. It becomes a sanctuary for growth, healing, and love. Embrace these practices with an open heart and watch as your family thrives in ways you never imagined possible.

Parent-Child Repair Scripts

How safe is it to be human in your home?

> "Emotional safety isn't the absence of conflict—it's the presence of connection, even when things get hard."

Use this worksheet alone or with a loved one to gently assess the emotional climate in your home and explore new patterns for deeper connection.

Section 1: How Emotionally Safe Does My Home Feel?

On a scale from 1 (Rarely) to 5 (Consistently), rate the following statements:

Statement	1	2	3	4	5
I feel safe expressing my emotions at home	☐	☐	☐	☐	☐
Conflicts in my home are repaired with care	☐	☐	☐	☐	☐
When someone in my home is upset, others respond with empathy	☐	☐	☐	☐	☐

I can ask for alone time without guilt	☐	☐	☐	☐	☐
I feel seen and valued even when I'm not doing or performing	☐	☐	☐	☐	☐
We have regular moments of meaningful connection (talks, meals, etc.)	☐	☐	☐	☐	☐
Apologies are offered without defensiveness	☐	☐	☐	☐	☐
I know what helps my loved ones feel emotionally safe	☐	☐	☐	☐	☐
Others in my home know what helps *me* feel emotionally safe	☐	☐	☐	☐	☐

Total Score: _____ / 45

36–45 = Emotionally rich and supportive

25–35 = Supportive with room to deepen

15–24 = Some disconnect—explore unmet emotional needs

Below 15 = Safety may feel inconsistent or conditional

Section 2: Reflect & Reveal

1. One way I currently contribute to emotional safety at home is:

2. One area I could grow in is:

3. One thing that would help me feel more emotionally supported is:

4. One thing I can offer to help *others* feel safer with me is:

Section 3: Choose 1-2 Supportive Actions to Practice This Week

☐ Initiate a check-in with a loved one ("How are you feeling lately?")

☐ Offer a "non-fixing" response to someone's emotions

☐ Create a device-free moment of presence (meal, walk, bedtime, etc.)

☐ Say: "I appreciate you for…" to someone in your home

☐ Repair a recent moment you handled poorly ("I wish I had responded differently—can we try again?")

☐ Ask a loved one: "What helps you feel safe and connected with me?"

Pro tip: *Choose just one action and do it consistently. Emotional safety grows through repetition.*

Raising Emotionally Resilient Children

Emotional resilience is learned, witnessed, and internalized. It is not inherited. Like a muscle, it strengthens through repeated experiences of safety, reflection, and recovery. If we shield our children from all discomfort, they miss the opportunity to learn how to navigate emotional challenges with support, curiosity, and self-trust.

Parents and caregivers play a vital role in shaping this process. Every moment of co-regulation, every patient response to a tantrum or a disappointment, teaches a child how to name their feelings, hold them without shame, and return to balance.

Naming Emotions Builds Regulation

Children often experience big feelings long before they have the language to describe them. Helping them build an emotional vocabulary—by labeling emotions in real time—gives them the tools to understand what's happening inside.

Instead of saying, "You're fine," try, "You look really frustrated right now—want to talk about it?" This communicates that emotions are valid, nameable, and worth exploring. Over time, children begin to develop the confidence to navigate their inner world without fear or repression.

Co-Regulation Is the First Step Toward Self-Regulation

Before children can regulate themselves, they learn to borrow your calm. When you remain grounded during their emotional storms, you become a safe harbor. Rather than pressuring yourself to have the perfect response, simply stay present when emotions run high.

Strategies such as using a calm tone, sitting beside them during distress, or modeling deep breaths can help shift their nervous system from a state of overwhelm to one of safety. Through repetition, children internalize these strategies and start using them independently.

Teaching Recovery, Not Perfection

Children don't learn resilience from flawless behavior; they learn it by watching what happens after the rupture. When they witness you make a mistake—and then apologize sincerely—they absorb an invaluable lesson: connection can be repaired.

In moments when you've lost patience or spoken harshly, own it. Say, "I was feeling overwhelmed and didn't speak kindly. I'm really sorry. Let's try again." These micro-repairs teach children that emotional missteps don't mean love is lost; they mean we're human, and we're learning.

Parent-Child Emotional Resilience Activity: "What Can We Do About It?"

A collaborative activity to help your child face challenges with confidence, flexibility, and support.

"Resilience isn't about never feeling upset— it's about knowing what to do next when you do."

Set the Scene

Choose a calm moment—after dinner, during a walk, or before bedtime

Have paper, pens, or crayons handy

Sit side-by-side or across from one another, not face-to-face like a test—this is about teamwork

Step 1: Choose a Real-Life Scenario Together

Pick a challenge your child has experienced recently. (Let the child choose, or gently offer options.)

Examples:

- "You didn't get picked for the team."
- "A friend said something that hurt your feelings."
- "You had to try something new and it felt scary."
- "You forgot something important and felt embarrassed."

Prompt:

"Let's write down or draw what happened in that moment."

Step 2: Name the Feeling, Not Just the Problem

"Every problem brings a feeling with it. Let's figure out what your feeling was trying to tell you."

Help your child name what came up:

- ☐ Embarrassed
- ☐ Angry
- ☐ Sad
- ☐ Frustrated
- ☐ Nervous
- ☐ Left out

Other:

Then ask:
"What do you think that feeling was trying to protect or tell you?"
(e.g., 'I wanted to feel included.' 'I wanted to feel confident.')

Step 3: Explore Healthy Coping and Solutions Together

Use the three-column method:

What I Can Think	What I Can Say	What I Can Do
"I'm learning."	"That hurt my feelings."	Take a break
"I can try again."	"Can I have help?"	Deep breaths
"This won't last forever."	"Let's talk about it."	Write or draw about it
"I don't have to be perfect."	"I feel _____ right now."	Hug someone I trust

Let your child choose or create one from each column. Draw them as "tools" they can keep in their pocket or backpack.

Step 4: Reflect and Reinforce

End with this dialogue prompt:

"What do you think you learned from that hard moment?"

"What helped you the most—me listening, us solving it together, or something else?"

And offer an affirmation:

"Even when things are tough, I see how strong you're becoming. I'm proud of the way you showed up."

Bonus: Create a "Brave Moment Jar"

Every time your child works through a hard feeling or challenge, write it down and drop it in a jar or box. Over time, this becomes a **visible archive of resilience**.

Encouraging Autonomy Within a Secure Base

Emotionally resilient children feel capable and supported. You foster this by offering choices, inviting collaboration, and encouraging problem-solving. Let them try and stumble, knowing they can come back to you for comfort and encouragement.

When children trust that they can express themselves without being shamed or silenced, and that mistakes are part of growth, they're more likely to face life's inevitable challenges with flexibility and confidence.

What builds emotional resilience over time isn't a single moment of praise or discipline but the day-in, day-out consistency of presence, attunement, and repair. When children grow up in environments where emotions are understood rather than dismissed, they develop inner strength and self-worth that lasts well into adulthood.

Challenge of the Week: Try Something New, Grow Together

Purpose:

To build family-wide emotional resilience by encouraging each member to try something that stretches them, followed by shared celebration and reflection—fostering connection and a lifelong love of learning.

Step 1: Choose Your Challenge *(Sunday or Monday)*

Each family member selects **one small challenge** they'll try this week. It should be something just outside their comfort zone, not overwhelming.

Sample Prompts:
- Try something you've never done before
- Speak up when you usually stay quiet
- Ask for help
- Learn a new skill
- Apologize or repair a relationship
- Try again after something didn't go well
- Say "yes" to something brave
- Let someone see your real feelings

Write your challenge here:

"This week, I'm challenging myself to:

Step 2: Track Progress Gently

Throughout the week, check in briefly:

What's feeling hard?

What are you learning about yourself?

Who or what helped you feel brave?

Step 3: Share & Celebrate Together *(End of Week—Friday or Saturday)*

Each family member answers:
- *Did I complete my challenge?*
- (If not, what stopped me? No shame—just awareness.)
- *What did I learn about myself?*
- *How did it feel to try something new—even if it didn't go perfectly?*
- *How can the family celebrate this effort together?*

(High five, dance party, special dessert, "bravery badge" stickers, etc.)

Closing Affirmation (Say Together):

"Trying is more important than being perfect. We grow when we stretch, and we're proud of each other for showing up with courage."

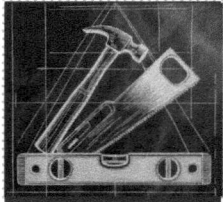

Fixed vs. Growth Mindset Praise for Parents

"Praise that focuses on effort and process helps kids see themselves as learners, not performers."

—Adapted from the work of Carol Dweck,
Mindset: The New Psychology of Success

Fixed Mindset Praise	Growth Mindset Praise
"You're so smart!"	"You worked hard to figure that out—great persistence!"
"You're really good at this."	"I can see how much practice you've put in—it's paying off."
"You're a natural at math."	"The strategies you're using are helping you improve—keep going."
"That was easy for you!"	"Let's find a way to stretch your brain a little more next time."
"You're just not a reader."	"Reading can take time to click—let's find a story that pulls you in."
"You got the highest score—awesome job!"	"What part of that did you feel proud of, and what did you learn from it?"
"You're always my best helper."	"I noticed how carefully you helped today—that kind of focus matters."
"Wow, you're really talented!"	"I saw how you kept trying even when it got tough—that's real skill."
"That drawing is perfect!"	"Tell me about how you made this—I can see the effort in the details."
"Don't worry, you're just gifted."	"Even when you're good at something, effort still helps you grow."

Pro tip for parents:

Ask follow-up questions like:
- "What part was hard?"
- "What did you learn about yourself?"
- "What would you try differently next time?"

These open up conversations about process, and encourage lifelong learning over performance pressure.

Bridging Generational Communication Gaps

For most of us, it doesn't take much effort to imagine a familial scene that demonstrates the intergenerational communication gap. Young family members sit on couches, glued to their screens, thumbs moving at lightning speed, while the seasoned company gathers in the kitchen to reminisce about days without Wi-Fi. But the differences can be even more subtle than that.

I had an experience recently at the office that highlighted this for me. My coworker's phone pinged on her desk as I drafted my next email. Not two seconds later, it pinged again. Then again. Then again. Then *again*. I looked over at her, email forgotten, and she seemed unfazed by the repeated pings.

"Someone really wants to get a hold of you," I said.

Without even turning away from her own keyboard, she replied, "No. That's just one of my younger friends, Mia. She's in her early twenties, so, you know, every thought is its own text. If it were one of my friends in their thirties or forties, I would be worried."

As a thirty-something paragraph texter, her keen observation struck me as a subtle but distinct difference in the way shared technology can be used by differing age groups. To me, the rapid pinging denotes urgency, but she knew to expect that would not always be the case with some of her younger connections. (I should note, this was an anecdotal observation and certainly not the case with every younger texter.)

Technological influences have widened the traditional chasm between intergenerational communication, but the root cause remains the same: differences in value systems and language use.

Case Study: The Ramirez Family—Bridging Generations Through Shared Purpose

"When they stopped trying to talk about everything and started creating something together, something shifted. Connection grew in the doing."

Background: A Growing Gap

The Ramirez family, a multigenerational Latino household, shared a home—but not always a shared understanding. Three generations lived under one roof in Phoenix, Arizona:

Elena (78, she/her): The matriarch, steeped in tradition, mainly spoke Spanish and valued hierarchy and respect.

Marisol (45, she/her): Her daughter, a first-generation American, was a busy school counselor who often acted as a cultural translator between her mother and her children.

Ava (17, she/her): Marisol's daughter, a Gen Z high school senior, identified as queer, was passionate about social justice, and communicated predominantly through memes, sarcasm, and Spotify playlists.

Despite their love, conversations often dissolved into tension. Elena felt ignored, Marisol felt pulled in every direction, and Ava felt misunderstood, especially when her grandmother's values clashed with her identity and views.

The Turning Point: A School Project Turned Healing Catalyst

Everything changed when Ava was assigned a project for her ethnic studies class:

> "Create a multi-generational story that captures your family's history through an oral, visual, or creative medium."

Rather than struggle through it alone, Ava proposed a collaboration with her mom and grandmother.

At first, Elena was skeptical, unsure what she could offer or whether her stories had any value. But when Ava began recording their conversations on her phone and translating their dialogues into both Spanish and English subtitles for a short documentary, something surprising happened.

Elena lit up, recounting stories of her childhood in Jalisco, her migration journey, the songs her mother sang while folding laundry, and the heartbreak of leaving family behind. Ava, who had previously only heard fragments of her family's past, began to see her grandmother differently.

> "Abuela wasn't judging me. She just hadn't been invited into my world," Ava said.

> "And I hadn't been invited into hers."

The Innovation: Story Meets Technology

Marisol helped shape the project into an intergenerational bridge:

- She added commentary connecting her mother's experiences to her own as a bicultural daughter
- Ava used TikTok-style editing to juxtapose clips from each generation
- Elena taught Ava how to make tamales on camera, while narrating memories from her youth

What began as a homework assignment became a family legacy project—a digital time capsule that honored all three women.

The Outcome: A New Pattern of Connection

After the documentary's classroom debut (which received a standing ovation), Ava printed stills from the film and framed them for her grandmother's room. Elena now proudly showed visitors the framed photo of her and Ava in the kitchen—forever caught mid-laugh.

> "We didn't need to agree on everything to feel close," Marisol reflected.
>
> "We just needed a way to see—and be seen—across the gap."

Key Takeaways: What Helped the Ramirezes Bridge the Gap

- Shared projects reduced the pressure of direct conversations, making space for natural connection
- Storytelling invited curiosity instead of correction
- Creativity made room for each generation's strengths (wisdom, perspective, tech fluency)
- Emotional safety grew through collaboration, not confrontation

Bridging these gaps is crucial for maintaining family harmony and fostering understanding. Teaching Grandma to text or explaining TikTok trends to Dad may help, but the ultimate goal is to promote mutual respect and empathy, ensuring that everyone feels heard and valued.

When each member feels as if they contribute to the shared narrative, weaving together a tapestry of experiences and wisdom, the connection becomes more meaningful than the sum of its parts.

Storytelling Prompts for Intergenerational Connection

"Stories are the maps we pass down—not just of where we've been, but of who we are becoming."

1. ***"Tell me about a time when you felt really proud of yourself as a kid."***

   Why it works: Reveals formative values, early challenges, and core self-beliefs.

2. ***"What was friendship like when you were my age? What made someone a good friend?"***

   Why it works: Highlights relational norms, emotional needs, and social context.

3. ***"Was there ever a time you did something unexpected or brave? What happened?"***

   Why it works: Encourages vulnerability and shared awe or admiration.

4. ***"Who was your first love—or someone you learned a lot from in love?"***

   Why it works: Opens the door to emotional memory and relationship wisdom.

5. ***"What was going on in the world when you were growing up? How did it shape you?"***

   Why it works: Places personal stories within historical or cultural context.

6. ***"What's a mistake you made—and what did it teach you about life or people?"***

   Why it works: Models humility and growth mindset across generations.

7. **"What's something you hope our generation holds on to from yours?"**

   Why it works: Creates a sense of legacy and mutual respect.

8. **"What's a memory that still makes you laugh every time you think about it?"**

   Why it works: Adds levity and shared joy to deepen connection.

Pro tip: After each story, ask follow-ups like:

"How did that moment shape you?" or "What do you think I can learn from that?"

A healthy family community's strength and support surpass that of its individual members, just as two yoked horses can pull the weight of three. This crucial interconnectedness serves as the backbone of resilience, allowing families to weather life's storms together.

How can one enhance intergenerational communication?

1. Practice Curiosity Over Correction

One of the most effective ways to bridge communication divides is through genuine curiosity. When you notice a generational habit that feels foreign or frustrating, ask questions that invite understanding:

"Can you tell me more about what that meant to you growing up?"

"What did you learn about emotions in your family?"

This helps family members feel seen in the context of their own upbringing, rather than judged by modern standards.

Encouraging storytelling can also be transformative. Let the youngest members share their exciting moments during playtime. Let your elders reminisce or recount family history. These narratives become the legacies that bind generations.

2. Normalize Emotional Literacy Across Ages

Older generations may have grown up in environments where emotional expression was viewed as a sign of weakness. They may not have had the language—or the safety—to talk about feelings. Younger generations, shaped by mental health advocacy and therapy culture, often speak more fluently in emotional terms.

Creating a shared emotional vocabulary takes time and patience. Model what emotional literacy looks like in everyday moments:

> "I felt really overwhelmed when that happened, and I could use some support."

This permits others to do the same, at their own pace.

3. Repair Matters More Than Agreement

Generational communication gaps may not always lead to mutual understanding, but they can still foster mutual respect. Focus on repairing the disconnection with empathy rather than trying to prove a point. Offer compassion for the limitations that shaped your elders, and space for younger generations to articulate new ways of relating.

When families witness one another's humanity—flaws, intentions, and growth—a sense of belonging deepens. It's okay to disagree across age lines. What matters is how you stay connected in the process.

4. Grow Forward Together

The goal is to honor differences while choosing connection. By creating safe spaces for storytelling, emotional expression, and vulnerability, families become living bridges linking the past with the future in real time.

At its core, bridging generational communication gaps means embracing both tradition and innovation. It's about sitting down for Sunday dinners where everyone's voice matters, and it's about incorporating digital tools that bring families closer. By valuing each generation's unique perspective, you create a family culture rich with diversity and depth.

So, gather your family—whether around a dinner table or on a group video call—and embrace the challenge of bridging generational communication gaps. With open hearts and minds, you'll find that these bridges not only connect ages but enrich lives in ways you never imagined possible.

Parenting Through Cultural and Societal Changes

Parenting has never occurred in isolation; a multitude of factors, including cultural, social, and environmental contexts, have always influenced it. From shifting gender roles to the rapid rise of digital technologies, today's families navigate a complex web of evolving cultural norms and societal expectations. What once felt like steadfast rules about parenting, discipline, or identity are now open to reevaluation. This is both freeing and overwhelming.

Modern parents often face a dual burden: honoring the values they were raised with while discerning which ones no longer serve their children's emotional well-being. At the same time, they're expected to respond to new concerns that didn't exist in prior generations: e.g., cyberbullying, mental health awareness, screen time limits, gender fluidity, global crises, and the ever-accelerating pace of change.

To raise emotionally healthy children in this context, adaptability and intentionality are key. Parenting in modern times requires more than keeping up with trends; it requires deeply tuning in to your child and to the larger world that is shaping their experience.

Raising Children in a Rapidly Evolving World

Children today are growing up in an era of unprecedented access to information and diverse influences. Social media offers exposure to diverse identities, ideas, and injustices, but also invites comparison, overstimulation, and fear. Cultural shifts around gender, race, climate, and equity are no longer abstract. They're present in classrooms, peer groups, and family conversations.

Emotionally attuned parents make space to process these realities. They ask questions like:

> "What are you hearing at school about this?"
> "How did that news story make you feel?"
> "What do you think is fair or unfair?"

These conversations foster emotional literacy, critical thinking, and moral development. They also send a crucial message: *You don't have to navigate this alone.*

The Role of Values in a Changing Landscape

As societal norms shift, your family's values can serve as both anchor and compass. Rather than rigid rules, values offer a flexible guide for parenting across change. Kindness, honesty, respect, and empathy, clearly communicated and embodied, help children build internal frameworks for decision-making in an often-unpredictable world.

Respect might look like listening deeply, not just obeying. Strength might mean vulnerability, not silence. Each generation has the opportunity—and responsibility—to parent in ways that match both the challenges and wisdom of their time.

Activity: Exploring Your Cultural-Emotional Blueprint

"Before we can choose how we relate, we must understand what shaped how we relate."

This activity can be completed individually, then discussed together as a family, couple, or group.

Step 1: Emotional Norms from Childhood

Reflect on your family or culture of origin. For each question, answer honestly:

1. **How were emotions expressed in your home growing up?**
   (e.g., were feelings talked about openly, kept private, shown through action?)

2. **What was your family's response to big emotions like sadness, anger, or fear?**
   (e.g., Were you comforted? Ignored? Told to toughen up? Reassured?)

3. **What messages (spoken or unspoken) did you receive about emotional needs?**
   ☐ It's okay to ask for help
   ☐ You should deal with things on your own
   ☐ Emotions are a sign of weakness
   ☐ Love means protecting others from your pain
   ☐ Other:

4. **How did people in your family show love or care?**
   (e.g., Words, food, presence, gifts, physical affection, acts of service)

Step 2: How Culture Shaped Attachment Beliefs

1. **What cultural values were emphasized in your home growing up?**
   - ☐ Respect for elders
   - ☐ Self-reliance
   - ☐ Obedience
   - ☐ Expressiveness
   - ☐ Community/family over self
   - ☐ Privacy/individual space
   - ☐ Harmony/avoiding conflict
   - ☐ Other:

2. **How did these values shape your beliefs about love, closeness, and boundaries?**

3. **Which of these values still guide you?** Which would you like to update or reframe?

Step 3: Create Your "Now" Blueprint

1. **What does emotional safety look like to *you* now, in your home or relationships?**

2. **When you feel connected, what is usually happening between you and others?**

3. **What new family value or emotional habit would you like to practice or pass on?**

   Example: "In our family, it's okay to cry."
   Example: "We take space when we need it—and we always come back."

Step 4: Share & Reflect Together

Use these prompts in a conversation with a family member, partner, or loved one:

- "One thing I learned about emotions growing up was…"
- "Something I didn't see modeled—but want to model now—is…"
- "I feel most supported when…"
- "What does love feel like in your culture? How do we blend that here?"

Practical Tools for Cultural Adaptability

- **Stay informed, but discerning**: Not every headline requires a reaction, but awareness helps contextualize your child's experience.
- **Model curiosity**: Let your children see you asking questions, exploring new ideas, and adjusting perspectives.
- **Encourage identity exploration**: Support your child's evolving understanding of who they are—in race, gender, interests, and beliefs.
- **Create a safe space for hard conversations**: Discuss complex topics openly and without shame. Silence often amplifies fear.

Families grow best in fertile soil where awareness, empathy, and emotional safety are consistently nurtured. In this chapter, we explored how conscious parenting, secure environments, generational bridges, and cultural sensitivity collectively shape the roots of resilience. Each interaction, from a bedtime check-in to a courageous conversation about social change, is an opportunity to model connection, safety, and adaptability.

But as many readers will recognize, family dynamics don't always start from a place of safety. Many of us carry wounds from our past—ruptures in our earliest relationships that still echo in our parenting and partnership today. To move forward, we must also look inward. In the next chapter, we'll explore how trauma impacts attachment and how healing becomes possible through compassion, self-awareness, and intentional repair.

05

Addressing Trauma and Healing

When I tuned into my body after that conversation with Paul, I felt something unexpected: a sense of peace.

Not relief, not triumph—just peace.

Because even though I couldn't control what Paul would choose next—whether he would show up for himself, for me, for our family—I chose to show up for myself. To speak what needed saying. To stay grounded in truth rather than fear. And that, in itself, was a radical shift.

Getting to that place takes work—deep, unglamorous, often painful work. It meant finally facing the old wounds I had long buried under logic and resilience. It meant addressing the trauma I carried from childhood, trauma that still whispered beneath the surface of my relationships, shaping how I loved and feared, connected and withdrew.

Paul and I both came from unconventional family systems: homes shaped by divorce, blended dynamics, and inconsistent emotional availability. The models we inherited weren't malicious; they were just incomplete. As a child, I grew up craving closeness but flinching from it at the same time. My home was often a battlefield, and I never knew which version of a loved one I would encounter. My disorganized attachment style took root early, wired for hypervigilance, constantly scanning for safety while aching for connection.

In my early twenties, Paul's steadiness felt like a sanctuary. He was grounded, hard-working, and dependable. I mistook his emotional distance for calm. I thought I had finally found someone immune to my fears. I didn't realize then that his self-reliance was a form of avoidant attachment—a protective shield he had built long ago, in childhood, when responsibility was thrust on him too soon.

At first, our differences balanced each other. When I leaned in anxiously or pulled away avoidantly, Paul barely reacted. He just stayed steady, unbothered, predictable. I thought it meant we were safe, even if I was often lonely.

Paul hit a personal crisis during the Pandemic that unraveled him from the inside out. His health declined. His confidence faltered. The emotional control he'd always relied on suddenly vanished. He became reactive, dysregulated, desperate for closeness—but still unable to tolerate vulnerability when it arrived. He'd pull me in, then push me away. I never knew which version of him I'd wake up to.

I gave all that I had to be the steady port during his storm so that he could return to himself, and, with considerable help and persistence, he did. Not without some sacrifices along the way.

In those years, he found every trauma landmine I had buried—and triggered them. Not maliciously, but undeniably. The woman I had worked so hard to become began to erode beneath the weight of trying to manage him, protect our son, and keep my own inner world from collapsing.

Something had to change.

I knew I could not outrun my pain or intellectualize my way out of it.
I had to confront the stories that shaped me.
I had to unlearn the love I thought I deserved.
I had to repair my attachment to myself.
And so I got to work.

I journaled. I breathed. I got honest with my inner child. I remembered the girl who had begged for love but learned to perform for survival. I held her. I gave her new words. I chose, moment by moment, to rebuild from the inside out.

Because survival was no longer enough.

Not for me. Not for my marriage. And certainly not for the child I was now raising.

THERE'S A MOMENT in every healing journey when you realize that what hurt you may not have been your fault, but healing it is your responsibility.

For many of us, attachment wounds and relational trauma are inherited quietly: passed through tone, behavior, silence, or rage. But there's good news—what was passed down can be transformed.

In this chapter, we'll explore how trauma shapes attachment and how it can be healed. You'll learn what it means to offer trauma-informed care to yourself and others. You'll reflect on emotional baggage not as shameful, but as instructive. And you'll begin to reclaim your narrative not by erasing the past, but by choosing what happens next.

Because healing isn't about forgetting what shaped you.
It's about finally becoming the author of your own story.

Recognizing Trauma's Impact on Attachment

"Solutions to problems in childhood often become problems in adulthood."

Trauma is not only what happened to you, but how your body and mind learned to survive. When trauma intersects with early caregiving, it shapes your core beliefs about safety, love, and trust. These patterns can reverberate throughout your life, particularly in how you form and maintain relationships.

Attachment isn't formed in a vacuum. It's forged through lived experience. If your early relationships were marked by neglect, volatility, enmeshment, or abuse, your nervous system adapted to protect you from these experiences. Adaptations like hypervigilance, emotional shutdown, people-pleasing, or avoidance are not inherently flaws. They're responses to environments that felt unsafe or overwhelming. Although these strategies once served a purpose, they can still interfere with connection long after the threat has passed.

Trauma, the Nervous System, and Attachment

When the caregiving environment is unpredictable or threatening, a child's nervous system learns to prioritize survival over connection. The stress response system (especially the amygdala, hippocampus, and HPA axis) becomes overactivated, making it difficult to regulate emotions, trust others, or feel secure in love.[55]

This chronic activation can lead to:

- **Hyperarousal**: feeling constantly on edge, easily triggered, and mistrustful
- **Hypoarousal**: feeling emotionally numb, detached, or checked out

- **Fragmented self-perception**: difficulty identifying needs or establishing boundaries
- **Relational instability**: fear of abandonment or engulfment, even in healthy dynamics

For individuals with disorganized attachment, which is often linked to unresolved trauma, relationships feel like both a lifeline and a threat. There may be an intense longing for closeness, immediately followed by the impulse to withdraw. This internal push-pull can make intimacy confusing, painful, and exhausting.

Making the Invisible Visible

One of trauma's most pervasive effects is invisibility. Survivors often minimize or forget what happened, especially if the trauma was chronic or relational (e.g., emotional neglect, parentification, or inconsistent caregiving). But the imprint lingers in emotional triggers, nervous system reactivity, or the repeated feeling that closeness never quite feels safe.

Trauma manifests in multiple variations. **Acute trauma** is the result of a singular, shocking event—the piercing abruptness of a car accident or the sudden, jarring loss of a cherished loved one. **Chronic trauma**, however, involves the relentless pounding of ongoing stressors, such as bullying that chips away at self-esteem over time or neglect that erodes the foundation of self-worth. Then there is **complex trauma**, arising from a mosaic of varied and repeated painful experiences, often rooted in the tender soil of childhood.

The healing journey begins with recognition:

- When you flinch at kindness or brace for rejection, ask: *Is this current or historical?*

- When you overfunction in a relationship, ask: *Who taught me I had to earn love?*
- When you struggle to trust, ask: *What parts of me are still protecting the child I once was?*

These inquiries aren't meant to place blame but to create insight. And insight is the first step toward transformation.

Activity: Tracing the Thread— Where Did This Pattern Begin?

This self-reflective writing activity helps you explore patterns of emotional avoidance or anxiety in your relationships—and uncover the past experiences that quietly taught those responses.

Step 1: Identify the Pattern

Think about a recurring behavior or emotional reaction that feels automatic in your relationships.

Use one or more prompts to name your pattern:
- "I tend to pull away when…"
- "I often feel anxious or unsure when…"
- "I shut down or change the subject when…"
- "I say I'm fine, even when I'm not, because…"
- "When people get too close, I feel like…"

Step 2: Track the Pattern Backward

Now ask: **"Where might I have learned this?"**

Think of moments in your early life—whether big or small—that mirror this feeling.

Use these guiding prompts:
- Was there a time I reached for emotional support and didn't receive it?
- Who taught me it was safer to hide what I feel—or not need anyone?
- Did I grow up walking on eggshells to avoid someone's reactions?
- Was love in my home conditional, unpredictable, or withdrawn?

Step 3: Understand What the Pattern Was Protecting

Now reflect:
- What was this pattern trying to help me avoid? (e.g., rejection, shame, conflict)
- What did it *achieve* for me at the time? (e.g., safety, belonging, invisibility)
- What did it cost me? (e.g., closeness, authenticity, trust)

Step 4: Invite a New Possibility

Complete the following:
- "This pattern helped me survive. But now, I want to…"
  - ☐ Trust more
  - ☐ Stay present
  - ☐ Speak up
  - ☐ Receive love
  - ☐ Something else: _____
- "What I needed then that I didn't get was…"
  (e.g., comfort, protection, validation)
- "What I can offer myself now is…"
  (e.g., self-compassion, new boundaries, safer relationships)

> **Closing Affirmation**
>
> *"The pattern is not who I am. It was my protector.
> I'm allowed to outgrow what once kept me safe."*

If you find yourself subconsciously or consciously avoiding intimacy or feeling heightened anxiety when people draw near, these could represent echoes of past traumas resonating within your present relationships. Emotional triggers, those seemingly innocuous moments when a casual comment suddenly sends you spiraling into an abyss of insecurity or anger, serve as subtle indicators. A therapist I once saw used to say:

If you're hysterical, it's historical.

These responses are not congruent with the present situation but are inexorably tied to unresolved traumas of bygone days, still echoing in the corridors of our minds.

The goal is acknowledging the presence and impact of trauma without becoming ensnared in the web of the past; illuminating the roots of your behaviors and gaining a fuller understanding of what shapes you. It's akin to finally mustering the courage to look under the bed for the monster that has kept you up at night, only to find harmless dust bunnies and forgotten socks. Building self-awareness and acceptance forms the first crucial step toward healing. Recognizing these ingrained patterns empowers you to choose new, healthier responses and nurture relationships that are fulfilling and grounded in authenticity.

From Survival to Connection

You're not fated to repeat the past. Recognizing trauma's impact on attachment means you can begin to repair it consciously. Therapeutic modalities such as EMDR, somatic experiencing, and internal family systems (IFS) help reconnect the mind and body, enabling you to respond to the present moment instead of reacting from the past.[77, 78]

Healing doesn't erase trauma—it rewires your relationship to it. Over time, with a safe connection, you begin to internalize new truths: *I can set boundaries without losing love. I can be vulnerable and still feel safe. I am worthy of a secure, mutual connection.*

Remember, in the intricate tapestry of life, trauma weaves itself with a complexity that can tangle and obscure the threads of our existence. However, with growing awareness and persistent effort, we possess the ability to untangle these knots, reweaving them into patterns that underscore our strength rather than accentuate disruption. By courageously acknowledging and recognizing the impact of trauma on attachment styles, you embark on the first valiant step toward profound healing and meaningful transformation, reclaiming the vibrant images of your life's tapestry.

Healing Attachment Wounds: From Emotional Baggage to Growth

Healing attachment wounds is about transforming the emotional and relational patterns that may have once protected you, but now get in the way of intimacy, safety, and trust.[7]

This emotional "baggage" isn't a sign of weakness. It's evidence of everything you've survived.

But survival is not the same as wholeness.
Emotional baggage often includes:

- **Unprocessed grief** from losses you were never allowed to mourn
- **Chronic self-doubt** rooted in childhood criticism or emotional neglect
- **Hyper-independence** that masks fear of rejection
- **People-pleasing** as a strategy to avoid conflict or abandonment
- **Emotional shutdown** from environments where your feelings were dismissed

These patterns usually form in childhood or early relationships and become default responses in adulthood. They aren't inherently bad, but when left unexamined, they quietly shape how you relate to yourself and others.[1]

The Healing Process: Rewiring the System

1. Build Emotional Range

Healing requires feeling. That includes discomfort, grief, joy, and tenderness. Start small: allow yourself to stay present with emotion rather than rushing to numb it. This helps you expand your capacity to experience life fully, without the emotional shutdowns that come from avoidance.

Mindfulness, body scans, and breathwork can support this expansion by grounding you during emotional intensity.[36]

2. Witness Without Judgment

Acknowledging the origin of your attachment patterns doesn't mean vilifying your caregivers. Many did the best they could with the tools they had. Naming the wound allows you to separate your current relationships from past survival strategies.

3. Track Your Triggers

Notice when your reactions feel disproportionate to the moment. A delayed reply from a partner might evoke panic or shutdown. These aren't overreactions; they're old reactions, reactivated. Journaling, somatic tracking, or therapy can help you map these responses.[55]

4. Make the Implicit Explicit

Many of our habitual emotional reactions stem from unconscious beliefs. For example:

- "If I set boundaries, people will leave."
- "If I express emotion, I'll be seen as weak."
- "If I'm not perfect, I won't be loved."

Once these beliefs are named, they can be challenged. You can begin to rewrite your inner script by gathering new evidence through safe relationships, healing practices, and repeated acts of self-trust.[86]

5. Practice Reparenting

Reparenting is the act of giving yourself the nurturance, boundaries, and emotional presence you needed as a child. It might look like:

- Soothing yourself during anxiety instead of seeking external validation
- Validating your emotions before analyzing or dismissing them
- Establishing boundaries that protect your nervous system

6. Seek Reparative Relationships

Attachment injuries heal in the context of safe, consistent, attuned relationships, whether with a partner, friend, therapist, or support group. Every moment of being heard, held, and honored begins to rewrite the internal script that says you're unworthy or unsafe.[84]

7. Repair When Rupture Happens

You cannot heal attachment wounds by avoiding close relationships. You need to learn how to fix things. This means admitting when you are wrong, taking responsibility, and working to rebuild trust. Each time you successfully repair a relationship, it shows that connections can survive mistakes.

8. Stay Inquisitive

On a regular basis, ask yourself:

- When do I feel the most insecure, unseen, or fearful in relationships?
- Can I identify what these moments remind me of from my early experiences?
- What would it look like to respond with care instead of criticism?

9. Create a New Emotional Blueprint

Decide what safety, trust, and connection look like now—not just what they used to require. Small examples of growth:

- Voicing a need and surviving it
- Taking a breath before reacting
- Asking for a hug instead of withdrawing
- Letting someone comfort you without apology

Each new behavior rewrites the story your nervous system once had to live by.

10. Create Meaning from Your Story

Growth involves reclaiming authorship of your narrative. Instead of defining yourself by what happened to you, explore how those experiences shaped your values, empathy, or strength.

Post-traumatic growth doesn't deny suffering but honors it. And finds new life on the other side.

Some people become parents they never had. Others create a relationship they never saw modeled. Some use their wounds to hold space for others.

This isn't toxic positivity—it's reclamation.

> *"The hurt doesn't become the point. But healing becomes the legacy."*

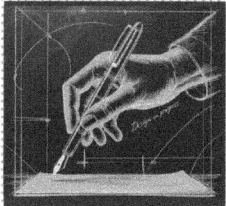

Activity: Rewriting the Story of Rejection

"Rejection hurt because you were wired for connection. But that pain doesn't get to be the author of your future."

Step 1: Name the Fear Without Shame

Begin by answering the following in a journal or aloud:

What does rejection feel like in your body?

(e.g., heart racing, heat in chest, stomach drop, tight throat)

When was a time I felt rejected and it really stayed with me?

(Briefly describe the event)

What did I make that rejection mean about me?

(e.g., "I'm too much," "I don't matter," "I'm not lovable")

Important note: Rejection *hurts* because your brain and body are wired for social belonging. It's a protective wound, not a personal failure.

Step 2: Distinguish Risk from Identity

Next, challenge the emotional narrative:

- Was that rejection about me—or about their capacity, timing, or understanding?
- Have I ever rejected something or someone *not because they weren't worthy*, but because I wasn't ready?
- What part of me is still trying to prove I'm worth keeping?

This step begins to separate self-worth from outcome—a foundational piece of emotional resilience.

Step 3: Soothe the Body's Rejection Alarm

When the fear of rejection is triggered, your amygdala sounds an alarm. You can practice calming it with somatic tools. Try this grounding exercise next time you feel fear rising:

"Hand to Heart + Breath Work" (3 minutes)

- Place one hand on your heart, the other on your stomach.
- Breathe in for 4 counts, hold for 2, breathe out slowly for 6.
- Whisper: *"I am safe even when I feel scared."*

Repeat until the wave softens. Then proceed.

Step 4: Take a Micro-Risk Toward Connection

Rebuilding resilience requires small, safe exposures. Choose one of the following mini-reconnection practices:

- Text a friend just to say you appreciate them
- Share a vulnerable truth in a low-stakes setting (e.g., "I've been struggling a bit lately")
- Make a light request (e.g., "Can we talk later? I'd really like your support.")

Afterward, reflect:

- What did I fear might happen?
- What actually happened?
- What did I learn about myself in the process?

Even if the response wasn't perfect, remind yourself: the practice is in the asking, not the outcome.

Step 5: Write a New Narrative

End the activity by completing these prompts:

- "I used to believe rejection meant…"
- "Now I'm learning it might also mean…"
- "When fear rises again, I'll remind myself…"

Example:

"I used to believe rejection meant I was unworthy. Now I'm learning it might mean the fit wasn't right—and that doesn't erase my value."

Optional Affirmations

- "Not everyone has to choose me for me to be enough."
- "Their no does not define my worth."
- "I'm allowed to be seen and still feel safe."
- "I can handle discomfort without abandoning myself."

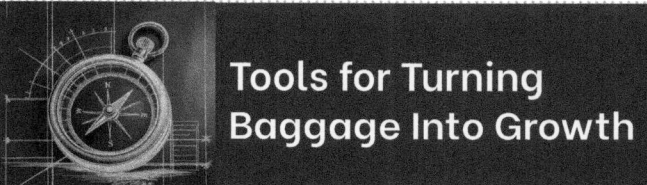

Tools for Turning Baggage Into Growth

- **Journal Prompt:** "What old belief am I still carrying that no longer serves me?"
- **Practice:** Notice one moment this week when you felt the pull of an old pattern. Pause. Choose differently, even if just slightly.
- **Mantra:** "I honor what I had to carry. But I get to choose what I hold now."
- **Conversation Starter:** "Can I share something I'm working on from my past, so you can understand how I'm trying to grow?"

You are not broken. You are adaptive, shaped by your circumstances, and capable of rewriting the story you've inherited. With intention and care, your emotional baggage can become a source of wisdom, empathy, and resilience.

Trauma-Informed Care: Principles and Practices

"When we shift from asking 'What's wrong with you?' to 'What happened to you?'—we stop diagnosing pain and start honoring it."

Many attachment wounds begin when someone's needs are ignored, punished, or misread, especially in early caregiving relationships. Trauma-Informed Care (TIC) offers an opportunity to rewire those experiences through safe, attuned interactions that send a new message:

"You matter. You're allowed to feel. And I will not leave you in your pain alone."

Whether in a therapy office, classroom, doctor's office, or kitchen table, trauma-informed care allows us to repair trust at the root and model a new, safer world for ourselves and each other.

Beyond being a therapeutic technique, TIC is a paradigm shift in how we see people and their pain. The concept first gained traction in the early 2000s through the work of researchers and clinicians like Dr. Sandra Bloom and the Substance Abuse and Mental Health Services Administration (SAMHSA). It was a response to a growing realization: many clients seeking services—medical, mental, educational—had experienced trauma that shaped how they accessed care.

Too often, systems designed to help inadvertently re-traumatize individuals by ignoring the emotional, relational, and neurobiological effects of trauma.

Trauma-Informed Care emerged as a framework to change that. It asks us not only to recognize the prevalence of trauma, but also to adapt our systems and relationships to create emotional safety, trust, and choice. TIC invites a deeper awareness of how trauma impacts the body, mind, and relationships, and how healing happens best in environments that feel safe, empowering, and collaborative.[79]

At its core, TIC is built around five core principles:

1. Safety
   Emotional and physical safety is foundational. A trauma-informed space prioritizes non-judgment, consistency, and calmness. Survivors must feel safe to let their guard down, not pressured to.

2. Trustworthiness and Transparency
   Trust is rebuilt through small, consistent actions. Being clear about intentions, expectations, and boundaries helps survivors regain a sense of control and predictability.

3. Choice and Autonomy
   Trauma can make a person feel powerless. Offering choices—whether in conversation, treatment, or daily routine—restores agency. Even small acts of choice can be profoundly healing.

4. Collaboration and Mutuality
   Healing is not something done to someone but built with them. Collaboration creates a dynamic where survivors are seen as active participants in their healing, not passive recipients of care.

5. Empowerment and Strengths-Based Support
   Rather than focusing on deficits or dysfunction, TIC highlights resilience. Survivors have already found ways to survive. Now, they're building new strategies to thrive.[80]

Some frameworks also include:

- **Cultural, Historical, and Gender Responsiveness**—honoring identity-based trauma

- **Resilience & Recovery Orientation**—seeing individuals as capable of healing, not defined by their trauma

These principles guide how we respond to behaviors, emotions, and needs, especially those that might otherwise be labeled as "difficult" or "resistant."

A trauma-informed lens doesn't ask "Why are you reacting like this?" It asks: "Could this be a survival response?"

Core principles of TIC guide its practices with precision and empathy. Collaboration and mutuality stand at the forefront, emphasizing partnerships between caregivers and those they serve. In this dance of healing, both parties contribute equally, fostering a sense of shared goals and mutual respect. Empowerment and choice are equally critical; individuals are encouraged to take ownership of their healing process, making decisions that align with their values and aspirations. This collaborative approach ensures that healing isn't imposed but co-created, nurturing a genuine sense of agency and autonomy.

Trauma-informed care is now used across many environments:

- **Mental health and medical care**
  e.g., recognizing trauma histories when treating chronic pain or anxiety

- **Education**
  e.g., offering calming spaces for dysregulated students rather than punishment

- **Workplaces**
  e.g., training managers to recognize signs of burnout and secondary trauma

- **Social services and child welfare**
  e.g., avoiding coercive interventions with vulnerable youth

- **Correctional and legal systems**
  e.g., offering therapeutic alternatives to incarceration

- **Family and parenting dynamics**
  e.g., replacing shame-based discipline with curiosity and co-regulation

Even couples and friendships can become trauma-informed when partners learn to regulate, repair, and respond with attuned empathy rather than assumptions.

While TIC is a philosophy, it is often supported by specific techniques, including:

- **Grounding and mindfulness** (to help regulate the nervous system)
- **Strengths-based language** (focusing on what's working, not just what's broken)
- **Choice and consent in interactions** (e.g., "Would you like to talk now or later?")
- **Psychoeducation** (about trauma's impact on the brain and body)
- **Reflective listening and validation** ("That makes sense given what you've been through.")
- **Body awareness and somatic safety tools**
- **Attachment-based repair work** (in relational settings)

What matters most is not the tool itself—but the way it's offered: slowly, gently, and always with emotional permission.

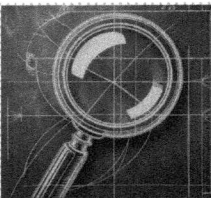

Case Study: Jordan— Healing Attachment Wounds Through Trauma-Informed Care

"I kept thinking I had to earn love by shrinking myself. Now I'm learning that being loved means being seen."

Background: The Early Blueprint

Jordan (he/him), a 29-year-old gay man, entered therapy seeking relief from chronic anxiety in relationships. Though outwardly confident, successful in his career as a graphic designer and socially active, he described an invisible exhaustion: constantly monitoring others' moods, over-apologizing, and feeling emotionally abandoned even in close friendships or romantic partnerships.

From an attachment perspective, Jordan's pattern reflected anxious-preoccupied attachment, shaped by a childhood marked by inconsistent caregiving and emotional invalidation.

Growing up in a conservative religious household, Jordan learned early that his emotions—and identity—were sources of disconnection and danger. When he cried or expressed sensitivity, he was told to "man up." When he tried to come out at 15, his parents responded with silence, shame, and the threat of disownment. While he maintained a surface-level relationship with them into adulthood, Jordan had internalized a message:

"Love is conditional. You must earn it by being less of yourself."

Therapeutic Approach: Trauma-Informed Foundations

Jordan's therapist, trained in trauma-informed and attachment-based modalities, emphasized from the beginning:

- **Emotional safety**: Jordan could go at his own pace, without pressure to disclose.
- **Transparency and collaboration**: The therapist explained each approach and invited Jordan to choose what felt right.
- **Empowerment**: Jordan's identity wasn't just accepted—it was affirmed as a strength, especially in the context of his resilience.
- **Curiosity over correction**: When Jordan would self-blame ("I must be too needy"), the therapist responded not by disputing it—but with warmth and inquiry:

"Where did you first learn that needing someone meant being too much?"

Key Healing Moments: From Shame to Securement

Over time, Jordan began to explore how his early attachment wounds and cultural trauma intertwined. Some key insights and moments of healing included:

1. Unpacking the Protector Parts

Jordan realized his over-functioning in relationships (e.g., checking in constantly, fearing disconnection) was a survival strategy rooted in his youth. As a teen, he had become hyper-attuned to others' moods to avoid rejection.

With compassion, he began to say:

> *"This anxiety isn't me being broken; it's the part of me that tried to keep love from leaving."*

2. Regulating the Nervous System

With somatic exercises and grounding techniques, Jordan learned how to recognize the physical signs of a triggered attachment wound (e.g., tight chest, racing thoughts, stomach discomfort) and respond with self-soothing tools, rather than spiraling into shame.

Breathwork, bilateral tapping, and short affirmations like

"I'm safe now; I don't have to chase love" became part of his healing practice.

3. Practicing Secure Language

The therapist introduced examples of secure attachment language, which Jordan practiced with friends and, eventually, with his new partner:

- "I'm feeling a bit disconnected and would love some reassurance. Can we talk?"
- "When you didn't text back, I noticed my mind went to old fears. I'm working on this and wanted to name it."

Instead of fearing his needs would scare people away, Jordan learned that clear, kind expression could invite deeper intimacy.

Outcome: What Trauma-Informed Care Helped Achieve

After 14 months of therapy, Jordan reported:

- Less hypervigilance in romantic relationships
- A deeper sense of self-worth not dependent on others' approval
- More ease in setting boundaries with family and navigating difficult conversations about identity
- A felt sense that his needs weren't a burden; they were a bid for connection

Perhaps most powerfully, Jordan described this internal shift:

*"I'm not chasing people to fix something in me anymore.
I'm inviting them into something I value—and that includes me."*

Incorporating TIC into daily life requires intentionality and commitment. It involves recognizing the power dynamics inherent in relationships and striving for equity in every interaction. Whether you're a professional working with clients or an individual seeking personal growth, adopting these principles transforms how you engage with others and yourself.

Grounding Techniques Exercise

Take a moment to explore grounding techniques that can be integrated into your routine. Find a quiet space where you can sit comfortably, feet planted firmly on the ground. As you breathe deeply, focus on the sensations of your body. Feel the weight of your feet pressing into the floor, the texture of your clothing against your skin, or the rhythm of your heartbeat. Let these sensations anchor you in the present moment, providing stability amidst life's uncertainties.

Embrace these practices as flexible tools that adapt to your needs. Trauma-informed care empowers individuals with choice; it invites you to select what resonates most deeply with your journey. By fostering environments where safety, trustworthiness, and empowerment reign supreme, we lay the groundwork for healing that is not only transformative but profoundly liberating.

TIC-Inspired Partner Activity: "What Helps Me Feel Safe with You"

To create a supportive, regulated space where each partner can explore and express what safety, connection, and trust feel like in their body and relationships.

Set the Scene: Safety First

- Choose a time when neither of you is distracted or emotionally activated
- Sit side-by-side or face-to-face in a calming space (a couch, a blanket fort, outside on a walk)
- Agree on a signal either partner can use to pause (e.g., raising a hand, saying "timeout")

Step 1: Reflect Independently

Each partner takes a few minutes to write down or think through the following:

1. **"I feel safest with you when…"**
   (e.g., you sit beside me quietly, you hold my hand, you ask how I am without rushing me)

2. **"When I'm upset, what helps me most is…"**
   (e.g., space to breathe, gentle touch, being asked if I want support)

3. **"Sometimes I shut down or react because…"**
   (e.g., I get overwhelmed, I fear being judged, I don't know what I need yet)

4. **"A supportive phrase I'd love to hear from you more often is…"**
   (e.g., 'You're not alone,' 'I'm here,' 'You don't have to explain right now')

Step 2: Share and Reflect Together

Take turns reading your reflections aloud. The listener should practice:

- Eye contact (if comfortable)
- Nodding and open body language
- Saying:
  » "Thank you for telling me."
  » "That helps me understand you better."
  » "Would you like a hug or some quiet time now?"

Do not offer advice or corrections. Just hold the space.

Step 3: Co-Create a "Safety Ritual"

Based on what you shared, co-create a small habit or ritual to build emotional safety between you. Examples:

- A "check-in" moment every Sunday evening
- A hand squeeze to signal "I'm here with you"
- A shared phrase for when emotions run high, like "Let's go slow together"

Optional Bonus: Body Co-Regulation Practice

Try 2-3 minutes of co-regulating touch or stillness, such as:

- Sitting back-to-back and focusing on shared breath
- Holding hands while silently noticing your heartbeats
- Sitting in comfortable silence, then whispering one affirmation to each other (e.g., "You're safe with me")

Post-Activity Reflection

Each partner can journal or talk about:

- "One thing I learned about you tonight..."
- "One way I want to show up differently for us..."
- "What safety now means to me..."

Reclaiming Your Narrative: Empowerment Through Healing

The Power of the Story We Tell Ourselves

We all live by stories: narratives formed from early experiences, repeated patterns, cultural messages, and the roles we were taught to play. These inner stories shape how we see ourselves in relationships, how we respond to conflict, how we define love, and most crucially, how we believe we are *allowed* to be.

Sometimes, these stories were whispered into our ears when we were too young to question them:

"You're too sensitive."
"You always have to be the strong one."
"If you need too much, people will leave."
"You're hard to love."
"You don't matter."

Over time, these statements become scripts—automatic beliefs that quietly dictate our relationships, boundaries, and sense of worth. And when trauma or insecure attachment reinforces those stories, they can begin to feel like truth.

But what if they're not?

The Brain's Role in Narrative Formation

Our brains are meaning-makers. When something painful happens, our minds look for an explanation, especially in childhood.

A constant cause-and-effect analysis is crucial to understanding the world when children enter it. This is how babies learn to open their mouths when approached with a spoon full of food, or how toddlers learn that saying "please" is more likely to result in a replay of their favorite song. It is also how children can learn that a tantrum might delay bedtime and get their caregiver to read another story, or how hitting their sibling might reward them with that toy they didn't want to share.

And the greater the effect, the more memorable the cause. Like placing a hand on a hot stove (usually a mistake only made once). Or being reprimanded by a parent.

A child's world is fairly simple: there's the world, and the world's ruler (aka their primary caregivers), and them. They don't know yet that their world's ruler is fallible. Everything that happens, happens for a reason.

So, what happens when the world ruler acts in a manner that is undeserved or unrelated to the child? For example, when the child is making playful noises and the caregiver, who is utterly exhausted from a frustrating work day, yells at the child to be quiet? The child was playing and, objectively, did nothing wrong. The caregiver simply took out their frustrations on the child.

When this happens, will the child assume the caregiver is wrong?

When you were little and your world was small, what was easier to believe—that the world was wrong, or that you were?

And so, without guidance, children often turn pain inward:

> "If I was treated this way, it must mean something is wrong with me."

These interpretations often become neural pathways, rehearsed over years until they feel instinctive.

Reclaiming your narrative requires consciously rewriting the meaning we attach to these past experiences.

Reclamation Is a Radical Act

To reclaim your narrative is to step into agency—to say:

> "I am not defined by how I was once treated."

> "I can choose how I respond, even if I didn't choose what happened."

> "I am allowed to see myself in a new light, even if others still expect the old me."

This is personal, and it can also be revolutionary, especially for those who have been marginalized, silenced, or dismissed.

Before rewriting, you must recognize what you're working with. Look for these signs:

- You hear a familiar inner voice in conflict: "This is all my fault."
- You feel the urge to shrink, over-explain, or silence your needs.
- You sabotage opportunities that feel "too good" because they don't match your self-story.
- You cling to roles that no longer fit (e.g., rescuer, caretaker, people-pleaser) out of habit or fear.
- You define yourself more by survival than by agency.

These are not flaws. They're old stories asking to be updated.

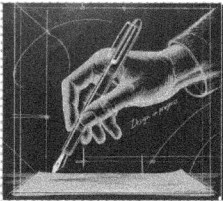

A Framework for Narrative Healing

1. **Name the inherited story**
   - » What belief about yourself keeps showing up in moments of vulnerability?
   - » Who (or what experience) taught you this story?

2. **Honor the protective purpose**
   - » How did this belief help you survive or stay safe?
   - » What did it protect you from feeling, facing, or losing?

3. **Challenge the distortion**
   - » Is this story true for who you are *now*?
   - » Is it based on outdated roles, trauma, or other people's limits?

4. **Reauthor with compassion**
   - » What would your most self-compassionate self say instead?
   - » What's a new narrative that allows for softness, courage, and growth?

Example:

Old story: "I always mess things up."
New narrative: "I've made mistakes, like everyone—but I am learning, worthy, and allowed to grow."

Tools to Support Narrative Reclamation

- **Journal prompt**: "What part of my story am I ready to reclaim?"
- **Mantra**: "My past shaped me, but I choose the next chapter."
- **Visualization**: Picture yourself stepping out of a costume labeled "Too Much" or "Unworthy" and into your true self
- **Dialogue prompt with a trusted person**: "Can I share a belief I'm trying to change about myself?"

Reclaiming your narrative doesn't mean forgetting what you've been through. It means saying:

> "This happened. And I'm still becoming. And I get to write who I am now."

Because healing is not erasure—it's evolution.

And you, dear reader, are allowed to become someone freer than your wounds ever imagined.

Notes:

06

Navigating Modern Relationship Challenges

There was a long stretch of time after that warm afternoon in my brother's condo when Paul and I felt more like project managers than partners.

We were both working full-time, trying to be good parents, and holding onto the version of ourselves we were slowly and carefully rebuilding. But with daycare pickups, deadlines, doctor appointments, and meal prep, connection no longer happened naturally. If we wanted time together, we had to schedule it. If we wanted to talk, we had to plan for it. Every point of contact, whether in-person or digital, had to be intentional.

So, we made rules. Rituals. Little anchors in the whirlwind.

We established a weekly date night and treated it like a sacred appointment. That two-hour window became something we protected fiercely. Sometimes it was quiet and cozy, sometimes intense, sometimes filled with laughter and reconnection, always important.

We prioritized therapy, too. We showed up to every session we could, even when we were tired or overwhelmed. I kept bringing honesty into the room, whether gentle or sharp. Paul kept showing his effort in quiet, deliberate ways.

One day, after a particularly vulnerable session, I returned home to find a handwritten note on my desk. Just a few lines:

> *"I wanted to tell you I love you. I know I can be challenging, and that things have been tough for a while. However, I am thankful for you and your love and strength every day."*

That note is still on my desk today, years later. And Paul knows it's there—because I told him. Because I've learned that effort only becomes intimacy when it's recognized. And because he needed to know his love was landing.

Things weren't perfect. The effort was real—but so was the exhaustion. We'd lose momentum. Life would throw curveballs. Some weeks, we felt in sync; other weeks, we drifted. But even in the harder stretches, there were these unexpected reminders that we were still choosing each other.

Like the day I walked into Paul's office, irritated after a tense exchange, and glanced at his monitor. In the bottom corner, taped like a quiet vow, was a sticky note that read:

> *"Fight for Helen every day."*

I stood there, stunned.

It didn't fix everything. But it reoriented me.

Even when I felt forgotten or under-prioritized, he had not forgotten what mattered. And that reminder softened something inside me.

Still, the digital age added its own layer of complication.

Paul's new photography hobby, which rekindled his energy and provided him with a sense of play he had long lost, required him to spend hours on his phone editing photos or scrolling for inspiration.

Sometimes I'd see him immersed in his screen and feel the old ache return; he's here, but not with me.

One day, after brushing off his phone use for the hundredth time, I logged into my dusty social media account just to feel a little closer to his world. What I found surprised me: dozens of memes, posts, and reels he had sent me over the past few months. Things that made him laugh or think of me. Sweet. Silly. Tender.

I thought I had been invisible. I wasn't. I was everywhere in his world—I just hadn't known where to look.

And his photography? It turned out to be one of the most unexpected gifts to our intimacy. Through his lens, I got to literally *see myself as he saw me. Not just in flattering light or beautiful composition, but in the way he noticed the quietest parts of me: the curve of a smile I hadn't realized I still had, the expression I wore when watching our son, the softness he still found in me after all we'd been through.*

We weren't the same people as when we met. But in many ways, we were learning how to love each other better—not despite the complexity, but through it.

MODERN RELATIONSHIPS are full of paradoxes: we crave closeness, but also autonomy. We live both online and offline simultaneously. We're pulled in a dozen directions yet still expected to show up with depth and grace for the people we love.

Thankfully, a secure connection isn't about keeping everything perfect. It's about staying *present*, even when life is loud. It's about communicating clearly, supporting each other through changing seasons, and creating meaning even in the mundane.

In the next chapter, we'll explore the realities of modern love: how technology, shifting gender roles, career demands, and emotional labor all intersect with attachment. You'll gain tools for navigating conflict, balancing independence and intimacy, and cultivating a lasting connection.

Because real love isn't about resisting change.

It's about growing together through it.

Digital Age Dynamics: Attachment in a Connected World

"We've never been more connected—or more unsure of where we stand."

In the digital age, our relationships unfold not only across kitchen tables and coffee shops, but also in texts, emojis, status updates, voice notes, and unread messages. Our phones have become both lifelines to connection and mirrors for our deepest insecurities.

Attachment dynamics don't disappear in digital spaces. In fact, they often amplify under the pressure of immediacy, ambiguity, and the constant presence of "other options." Where we once waited for handwritten letters or landline calls, we now carry the potential for validation—or rejection—in our pockets.

This blend of instant access and emotional uncertainty is shaping not just how we communicate, but how we *feel* in relationships.

Attachment Styles in the Digital Landscape

1. Anxious Attachment Online: Hypervigilance in the Feed
Anxiously attached individuals may become highly sensitive to:

- Delayed replies
- Changes in texting tone
- Social media activity (e.g., "Why did they like their ex's post but not reply to me?")
- Being left on "read" or seen

Their nervous system often interprets *silence* as *abandonment*, and digital ambiguity becomes a breeding ground for anxious spirals:

- "Did I say something wrong?"
- "Why didn't they heart that message?"
- "They used to reply instantly…"

This can lead to protest behaviors such as rapid texting, deleting messages, emotional withdrawal, or over-disclosing too soon.

2. Avoidant Attachment Online: Distance Without the Drama
While digital spaces may be more comfortable for avoidantly attached people, they can also be used for emotional distancing:

- Preferring texting to in-person vulnerability
- Ghosting rather than setting boundaries
- Ignoring emotional messages due to overwhelm
- Using humor or sarcasm to deflect closeness

The screen becomes a shield. When intimacy rises, avoidants may unconsciously create distance—*not* because they don't care, but because closeness feels like a threat to autonomy.

3. Disorganized Attachment Online: Mixed Signals, Real Pain
Disorganized attachment thrives in digital uncertainty:

- Alternating between intense connection and sudden silence
- Posting vague emotional messages to elicit care
- Being drawn to emotionally unavailable partners online

- Feeling unsafe in closeness *and* absence

Digital tools can become both a weapon and a wound used to test, provoke, or protect, often without conscious intention.

4. Secure Attachment Online: Clarity and Care

Securely attached individuals still feel hurt, longing, excitement, etc., but they approach digital communication with clarity, trust, and consistency:

- They respond mindfully
- They name needs without blame ("Hey, I'd love a check-in if you're busy")
- They don't make assumptions from silence, and they repair quickly if ruptures happen

Their presence online reflects their presence in real life: calm, caring, and reliable.

Modern Challenges in the Digital Attachment Era

*"Modern connection offers constant contact—
but not always consistent connection."*

With the simple act of tapping on a screen, physical and emotional distances diminish rapidly, and our anticipations soar to unprecedented heights. The ability to reach out instantly to someone on the opposite side of the globe is thrilling and full of potential.

Yet, this accessibility presents unique challenges, escalating expectations to respond instantaneously, creating unspoken pressure on both ends to keep the digital connection alive and buzzing. This intricate dance in the digital realm thus becomes a precarious equilibrium, carefully negotiated day by day, between the allure of accessibility and the imperative need for personal space.

While online communication undoubtedly offers unparalleled convenience, it does not come without its peculiarities and ambiguities:

- **Texting vs. Talking:** Digital communication can lead to misinterpretation. Without tone or facial cues, conversations risk an emotional disconnect. We often fill in the blanks with fear.
- **Social Media Comparisons:** Seeing others' highlight reels can trigger attachment insecurities—especially when partners don't post about you.
- **Dating Apps:** Swipe culture encourages replaceability, which can trigger abandonment wounds or avoidance under the guise of "endless options."
- **Digital Bread Crumbing:** Sporadic "likes," emojis, or flirty comments without follow-through can keep someone anxiously attached and emotionally entangled.

Digital interactions often strip down conversations to bare bones, missing the subtle nuances and emotional depth inherent in face-to-face discourse. This absence can sometimes leave us feeling isolated, even when a host of virtual companions ostensibly surround us. Consequently, the digital age conundrum emerges: how do we maintain healthy and meaningful attachments in a world teeming with digital distractions?

Attachments Within A World Of Instant Access

One pathway to nurturing attachments in the digital era is through the mindful establishment of boundaries, coupled with a deliberate focus on fostering substantive interactions. Begin by delineating clear limits for your online communication. Determine specific times and conditions under which you'll engage digitally to ensure uninterrupted quality time with the people you care about. Commit to spending time in face-to-face interactions, providing space for genuine connection to thrive, unimpeded by technological interference. Whether it's committing to a regular date night or planning a weekend retreat, prioritizing moments that cultivate true connection is crucial.

Furthermore, in the sphere of virtual relationships, there lies a tantalizing opportunity for connecting with a plethora of diverse individuals worldwide. You could be nurturing a friendship with someone residing in bustling Tokyo while comfortably lounging in your living room. However, while these virtual connections broaden our horizons, they sometimes risk becoming superficial or ephemeral, diverting attention from cultivating lasting, deeper bonds with those in our physical proximity. Striking a balance becomes key: embracing the global reach of digital interactions while cherishing the tangible connections with those who share your immediate life and environment.

What Healing Looks Like in a Digitally Connected World
"You are allowed to ask for emotional clarity—even in a world built on swipes, scrolls, and likes."

1. Name Your Triggers
   - ☐ "Seeing no reply makes my chest tighten."
   - ☐ "When I get short replies, I start feeling abandoned."
   - ☐ "I avoid checking texts because I fear demands."

2. Pause Before You Interpret
   Before spiraling, ask:
   - ☐ "Is this fact... or fear?"
   - ☐ "Do I have enough information to assume the worst?"

3. Communicate Needs Gently
   - ☐ "Can we talk about how we like to text when busy?"
   - ☐ "Would a check-in during the day help us feel more connected?"

4. Practice Digital Boundaries
   - ☐ Set intentional times to connect—not just constant access
   - ☐ Consider screen-free rituals or low-pressure catch-ups

5. Repair in Real Time
If something hurt you digitally, say so clearly:

> "When I didn't hear back, I felt unsettled. Can we talk about what happened?"

The tools we use to connect are not the problem. It's how we use them, how we interpret them, and how we repair through them that determines whether our digital lives deepen intimacy—or distort it.

Interactive Element: Digital Balance Checklist

To thoughtfully navigate this digital age, you can create and utilize a Digital Balance Checklist to evaluate and manage your digital interactions effectively:

1. Set Communication Boundaries: Clearly define when you're available for engaging in online chats and when your focus should wholeheartedly be on offline activities or in-person engagements.

2. Prioritize In-Person Time: Proactively plan and schedule regular face-to-face meetings or hangouts with your loved ones or close social circle to strengthen bonds.

3. Reflect on Virtual Connections: Regularly assess which online relationships genuinely enrich your life with quality interactions and which ones may drain your emotional or mental energy and should be adjusted or, if necessary, released.

4. Mindful Engagement: Cultivate the habit of being fully present during digital interactions; minimize the distraction of multitasking to enhance the quality of your engagement online.

By conscientiously finding and maintaining this delicate balance, you ensure that your relationships can thrive not just in the bustling avenues of the digital world but, more essentially, in the rich, fulfilling realm of real-world connections.

Balancing Independence and Intimacy: Finding Harmony

In today's achievement-driven culture, it's easy to feel like love and ambition are in competition. We're taught to hustle for success, chase stability, or prove our worth through performance. At the same time, our nervous systems crave safety, closeness, and belonging—things that don't show up on a résumé but shape our lives just as powerfully.

This conflict presents as both logistical and emotional. Managing career and relationship demands is about time, yes, but also identity, fear, and emotional safety.

Attachment Styles and the Work/Love Balance

1. Avoidant Attachment: Leaning into Work to Avoid Intimacy
Avoidantly attached individuals often channel energy into their careers because work feels predictable, rewarding, and controllable—unlike emotional vulnerability. They may:

- Stay late at work to avoid difficult conversations
- Prioritize independence over togetherness
- Feel smothered by relationship needs that compete with their professional goals

"Success makes me feel safe. Needing someone else doesn't."

2. Anxious Attachment: Leaning into Love, Sacrificing Self
Those with anxious attachment may put relationships above career, sometimes to the point of self-abandonment. They may:

- Downplay career aspirations to be more "available"
- Fear that ambition will lead to rejection
- Constantly seek reassurance that they're still loved or chosen

"If I focus too much on me, you might think I don't need you—and leave."

3. Disorganized Attachment: Torn Between Needs and Fears
Disorganized individuals often swing between extremes, craving closeness and fearing it, overworking and burning out, then withdrawing from both.

"If I try to do both, I'll fail at everything. If I do neither, at least I won't get hurt."

They may struggle to believe that they are *allowed* to pursue both success and connection without betrayal, abandonment, or collapse.

4. Secure Attachment: Integration Over Sacrifice

Securely attached individuals understand that career and connection aren't mutually exclusive. They:

- Communicate boundaries and needs clearly
- Offer and receive support without guilt
- See success as shared, not solitary
- Trust that their presence in the relationship isn't threatened by their growth or their partner's

"I can be ambitious and available. I can give love without losing myself."

How to Rebalance When Life Feels Off-Center

"Ambition and attachment can coexist—when neither is rooted in fear, and both are rooted in respect."

1. **Identify the Hidden Narrative**

Ask:
- "What do I believe I'll lose if I prioritize my relationship?"
- "What do I fear will happen if I focus on my career?"

These questions often unearth old wounds: being unseen, being minimized, being controlled. Once named, they can be challenged with compassion.

2. **Define Success on Your Own Terms**

Attachment security grows when we make intentional choices—*not reactive ones*. Define what success looks like in both areas of life:

- Emotionally: "I want to feel supported and seen."
- Professionally: "I want to grow without running myself into the ground."

Then ask: *"Where can both of these exist together?"*

3. **Have the Integration Conversation with Your Partner**

Sample prompts:

- "What does support look like for you when things get busy?"
- "What helps you feel like we're still connected when our schedules are packed?"
- "How can we celebrate each other's growth without feeling threatened or distant?"

This shifts the mindset from "career vs. love" to "we are teammates, not competitors."

You don't have to choose between building something for yourself and building something with someone else. The deeper work is learning to:

- Set boundaries with care, not fear
- Let yourself be supported, not saved
- Redefine productivity as something that includes joy, rest, and relational security

Partner Planning Guide: Balancing Career and Relationships

"Build a rhythm that supports both our ambitions and our bond."

Part 1: Reflect as Individuals First

Take a few quiet minutes to respond to the following questions on your own. This helps you approach the conversation with clarity and self-awareness.

1. How do I currently define success in my career?
2. How do I currently define success in our relationship?
3. When life feels busy, what do I most need to feel emotionally connected to my partner?
4. What makes me feel supported when I'm overwhelmed by work?
5. What's one fear or limiting belief I hold about balancing love and ambition?
   (e.g., "If I focus on my career, I'll be emotionally unavailable.")

Part 2: Share and Align Together

Set aside 30–45 minutes of uninterrupted time. Take turns sharing your responses. Be sure to listen from a place of curiosity over correction.

1. What are our busy seasons—times when one or both of us tends to feel overloaded?
2. What signs tell us when we're emotionally disconnected?
3. What does "being emotionally present" look like in practical terms for us?

Part 3: Design Our Shared Rhythms

Weekly Rituals of Connection

We will protect time for:

- ☐ Shared meal or tech-free check-in
- ☐ 15-minute "connection check" (How are we really doing?)
- ☐ Shared decompressing (walk, quiet time, cuddling, etc.)
- ☐ Other:

During Busy Times, We'll…

- ☐ Communicate anticipated stress before it spills over
- ☐ Set expectations for response time (texts, check-ins)
- ☐ Use a short phrase to signal need for connection or space (e.g., "refill moment" or "pause mode")
- ☐ Ask: "What would support look like for you this week?"

When Conflict Arises, We'll Try…

- ☐ Taking a pause, not a punishment
- ☐ Returning with curiosity, not criticism
- ☐ Naming the need beneath the reaction ("I felt dismissed" instead of "You don't care")

Part 4: Affirm What You're Building Together

Each partner completes:

"Something I admire about how you show up in your work is…"
"Something I appreciate about how you show up for me is…"
"A value I want us to hold onto—no matter how busy life gets—is…"

Closing Thought

You don't have to choose between love and purpose.

When you co-create your rhythm with intention and trust, you make space for both to thrive—together.

Redefining Relationship Norms: Beyond Traditional Expectations

"There is no single mold for connection. There is only what is chosen with care, with clarity, and with consent."

In recent years, the landscape of relationships has experienced a seismic shift, challenging age-old norms and redefining what constitutes a family. Gone are the days when the nuclear family was the sole model of relational success. Today, diverse family structures have emerged, each bringing its unique flavor to the mix. Single-parent families, blended families with stepparents and stepsiblings, and cohabitating couples who choose partnership without marriage are commonplace. This rise of non-traditional family setups reflects a broader acceptance of diverse relationship models, where love and commitment transcend societal conventions. The beauty of this evolution lies in the freedom it offers individuals to craft relationships that align with their values and needs, rather than conforming to pre-existing molds.

The benefits of redefining these norms are manifold. First and foremost, it grants people the autonomy to define relationships on their own terms. This newfound freedom means relationships can be tailored to fit the unique dynamics of those involved, fostering connections that are both genuine and fulfilling. By moving beyond rigid expectations, we embrace inclusivity and acceptance of diverse identities, allowing individuals to express their true selves without fear of judgment. This inclusivity enriches our communities, creating a tapestry of interconnected lives where authenticity thrives. In essence, by breaking free from traditional constraints, relationships become a reflection of personal growth and self-awareness.

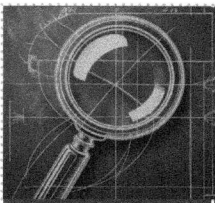

Case Study: Riley & Sam—Choosing Love on Their Terms

Background

Riley (32, they/them) was raised in a deeply traditional, religious household where love was measured by sacrifice, and marriage was considered the ultimate marker of maturity and success. Their parents modeled a highly gendered relationship—Dad as provider, Mom as caretaker—and any deviation from this model was seen as a failure or rebellion. Riley, a sensitive and expressive child, learned early that their emotions made others uncomfortable. They became attuned to others' needs, often at the expense of their own, a classic hallmark of anxious-preoccupied attachment.

Sam (38, he/him), in contrast, grew up in a household shaped by ambivalence. Emotional presence was unpredictable, particularly from his father, whose affection came only in short bursts between long absences or moments of tension. As a teen, Sam coped by developing a strong internal world, keeping people at arm's length, and relying heavily on his autonomy—a pattern consistent with avoidant-dismissive attachment. He was emotionally intelligent but guarded, and had long preferred casual relationships with low expectations.

The Inherited Beliefs They Carried

When Riley and Sam first met through mutual friends in a queer community arts space, there was an instant connection, but also unspoken pressure.

Riley quietly hoped this relationship would finally prove they were "mature" enough for a long-term commitment, something their family never believed possible without marriage.

Sam, on the other hand, feared losing himself in someone else's needs and wondered: "What if being deeply known means being controlled or abandoned?"

While their relationship was fulfilling in many ways, these inherited beliefs began to surface in moments of stress. When friends asked about wedding plans, Riley would smile on the outside but feel a pang of shame on the inside. Sam, sensing the emotional tension but unsure how to respond, would shut down or change the subject.

Neither of them wanted a conventional relationship. But they hadn't yet given themselves permission to build something intentionally different.

Bringing Attachment Awareness Into the Relationship

After a particularly painful evening in which Riley tearfully confessed, "Sometimes I feel like we're hiding in plain sight," and Sam responded, "I just don't want this to become something I can't breathe in," they decided to try couples therapy with an attachment-informed, queer-affirming therapist.

In therapy, they explored:

- Riley's internalized fear of being "too much," and how that linked to their anxious tendencies to over-accommodate or self-silence
- Sam's discomfort with expectation, and how avoidant defenses masked his underlying fear of disappointing someone he truly loved
- How both had unconsciously equated external validation (marriage, social milestones) with relationship legitimacy, despite wanting something more expansive and self-defined

Through this process, they began consciously restructuring their relationship, not as a default or a rebellion, but as a deeply chosen path.

How They Rebuilt Their Relationship on Intention

Together, Riley and Sam co-created what they called their Relational Blueprint, inspired by architecture and attachment theory alike. It included:

1. **Emotional Agreements:**
   "We tell each other the truth gently, even if it's messy."

   "We name needs before resentment builds."

   "We practice leaving space for complexity, especially when our reactions differ."

2. **Relational Structure:**
   A shared home with separate creative rooms ("intentional autonomy")

   A monthly check-in ritual where they reviewed goals, boundaries, and celebrated growth

   No wedding plans, but a private commitment ceremony on their fifth anniversary, where they exchanged letters—not rings—expressing how they choose each other in freedom and trust

3. **Reframing Commitment:**
   Instead of "forever," they chose a renewable commitment

   "We choose each other each year, with awareness, not assumption."

   They also introduced the practice of Relational Review Days—gentle, scheduled times to check in on their evolving values and adjust agreements as needed.

Where They Are Now

Riley no longer craves public milestones to feel legitimate. Instead, they say:

"The way Sam looks at me when we both keep a hard promise—that's what safety feels like."

Sam, once fearful of closeness, now initiates vulnerable conversations. He says:

"I realized I didn't want to protect myself from love. I wanted to protect the love we're building."

They still field awkward questions at family dinners and still feel pangs of doubt when comparison creeps in, but now, they have tools, language, and shared meaning. They are continuously practicing their relationship rather than performing one.

Final Reflection

Riley and Sam are not "anti-tradition." They are pro-intention. They didn't just rewrite the script; they co-authored it from scratch.

"What matters," Riley says, "is not how others define our love. It's how we live it."

A New Era of Relationships

For most of modern history, relationships followed a predictable script: find a partner, get married, stay together, raise a family—ideally for life. Cultural norms, religious beliefs, economic necessity, and rigid gender expectations largely shaped these roles.

But today, the landscape is changing. People are questioning:

- What defines a "real" relationship?
- Do we need to follow a timeline?
- Can we create emotional safety without living together?
- Is monogamy the only path to commitment?

What we're witnessing isn't chaos—it's conscious restructuring. More people are building their relationships around authenticity, emotional safety, and mutual consent, rather than social obligation.

And while this flexibility offers freedom, it can also stir anxiety, especially if your attachment blueprint was shaped by traditional models or relational trauma.

Attachment and the Pressure to Conform

Attachment patterns thrive on predictability and coherence. So when the relationship "rulebook" is no longer clear, our nervous systems may feel unsettled:

- The **anxiously attached** may worry, "If I don't follow the script, I'll never be chosen."

- The **avoidantly attached** may use ambiguity as an exit strategy: "If we don't label it, I can't get hurt."

- The **disorganized** may feel pulled in both directions: craving structure but fearing entrapment.

And even securely attached individuals may feel destabilized by a culture that prizes independence while also longing for connection.

For those exploring or considering alternative relationship models, communication becomes the cornerstone of success. Engaging in open dialogues about expectations and boundaries is crucial. In open relationships, for instance, discussing emotional needs and consent upfront can prevent misunderstandings and foster trust. Building a strong community support system is equally vital. Friends and networks that understand and respect your choices provide a sense of belonging, acting as a buffer against societal skepticism. Surrounding yourself with people who celebrate your relationship path empowers you to navigate challenges with confidence.

However, non-traditional relationships aren't without hurdles. Societal judgment often casts a shadow on those who deviate from the norm. Coping with this external pressure requires resilience and self-assuredness. Acknowledge that judgment often stems from misunderstanding; educate those willing to learn about your relationship dynamics. Additionally, ensuring mutual understanding and consent within your relationship is paramount. Regular check-ins help maintain alignment between partners' expectations, preventing potential rifts. Embrace open communication as an ongoing process. Relationships evolve, and so should conversations about them.

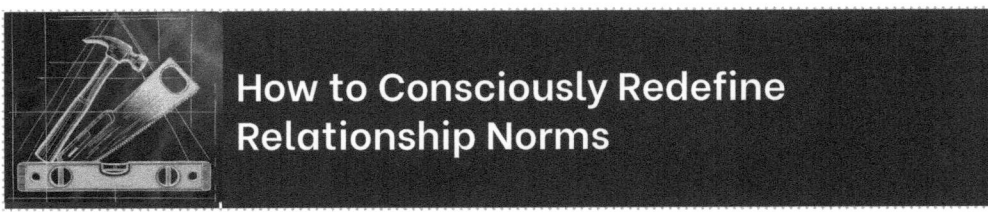

How to Consciously Redefine Relationship Norms

1. Define Your Shared Values

Ask each other:
- What do we want our relationship to *feel* like?
- What are the core values we want to honor? (e.g., freedom, loyalty, growth, curiosity)
- How do we want to make decisions together—intuitively, practically, democratically?

2. Challenge the Scripts You've Inherited
- Where did your ideas about love, timelines, or roles come from?
- Are they still true for you? Or are they rooted in fear, shame, or approval-seeking?

3. Communicate Expectations—Even Nontraditional Ones

Every relationship needs clarity. Don't assume your partner knows what "commitment," "freedom," or "future" means to you. Define it together.

4. Normalize Flexibility

Your relationship may look different over time. Kids, careers, relocations, or inner growth may reshape what works best. Revisit agreements like you would renegotiate a contract.

Rethinking the "Right Way" to Love

Let's name the traditional expectations often internalized—but rarely questioned:

- There's one person out there for me.
- Love means exclusivity.
- If it's right, it should be easy.
- Marriage is the goal.
- Commitment = cohabitation + merging everything.
- Children are the natural outcome of long-term love.

These beliefs are not *wrong*—they are just *inherited*. And inherited stories are allowed to be rewritten.

The truth is: **you get to define your relational values.** And the goal isn't to rebel against tradition, but to build intentionally, based on emotional health, compatibility, and conscious choice.

As we navigate these uncharted waters of evolving relationship norms, remember that each choice is an opportunity for growth. Embrace the fluidity of modern relationships with curiosity and compassion, knowing that there's no one-size-fits-all approach to love and connection. Celebrate the diversity that enriches our lives and revel in the freedom to craft relationships that reflect your true self.

There is no single "correct" way to love. There is only this question:

Does the relationship you're building make space for the truest versions of you, both now and as you grow?

If the answer is yes, then you're not defying the rules. You're writing your own with courage, care, and connection.

Partner Reflection Worksheet: Designing Your Relational Blueprint

"Let's choose how we love, not just how we were taught to."

Part 1: Reflect Individually Before Sharing

Each partner should take time to reflect privately before discussing together.

1. What does a healthy relationship look and feel like to me?

2. What messages did I grow up with about love, roles, or commitment?

3. Which of those messages do I want to keep, and which am I ready to let go of?

4. What are my top 3 relationship values?

(Examples: Trust, freedom, presence, growth, honesty, creativity, security, playfulness)

5. What does commitment mean to me—emotionally, physically, practically?

Part 2: Explore Together

Set aside uninterrupted time to share your reflections. Listen with curiosity, not correction. Complete the prompts below as a team.

1. Shared Relationship Values

List your top shared values and describe how you'll honor them in practice.

- **Value #1**: _____
  How we'll honor this:

- **Value #2**: _____
  How we'll honor this:

- **Value #3**: _____
  How we'll honor this:

2. Our Structural Agreements

These are flexible agreements that can evolve over time. They define *how* you choose to be in relationship.

1. What type of relationship are we building?

2. (e.g., *monogamous, polyamorous, queerplatonic, evolving, exploratory*)

3. What living situation supports our connection best?

4. How do we want to handle finances, parenting, time together vs. apart?

5. How will we revisit and revise these agreements when life changes?

3. Our Emotional Agreements

Think of these as *relational guardrails*—guiding how you treat one another during calm and conflict alike.

1. When conflict arises, we agree to:

2. When one of us needs space, we will:

3. When one of us needs reassurance or emotional care, we will:

4. Our repair practice (when we hurt each other, unintentionally or otherwise):

5. How we maintain emotional closeness during busy or stressful times:

Part 3: Future-Facing Questions

This final step helps keep your blueprint alive and evolving—not static.

1. We will revisit our blueprint every...

2. (e.g., quarter, year, life transition)

3. One ritual we'll use to reconnect with each other intentionally is:

4. We define "success" in our relationship as:

Closing Affirmations

Each partner completes and shares:

"One thing I love about how we show up together is..."
"One thing I'm excited to build with you is..."
"I'm choosing this relationship not because I have to—but because..."

BONUS: Partner Conversation Starter

Secure Attachment

"I'd love to take some time together to reflect on what's working well in our relationship and where we can grow. Want to map that out with me?"

Anxious Attachment

"I really care about us, and talking through what we both need in this relationship would help me feel more grounded. Could we try something together that helps us feel even closer?"

Avoidant Attachment

"I'd like to check in about how we do relationships—at a pace that feels right for both of us. No pressure—just a chance to align."

Disorganized Attachment

"Sometimes I feel torn between wanting connection and needing space. Could we explore how we both experience closeness and make it feel safer together?"

The Role of Social Media: Impact on Emotional Connections

Social media has transformed our social landscape into a double-edged sword, shaping how we perceive and interact within relationships. On one hand, it amplifies every milestone, turning engagements, anniversaries, and even break-ups into public spectacles. Remember when anniversaries were private affairs, celebrated quietly with loved ones? Now, they're grand productions with hashtags and curated photo albums. This magnification of personal moments can cultivate a sense of shared joy but also foster an unwelcome comparison culture. Scrolling through feeds filled with seemingly perfect relationships can erode self-esteem, leaving you wondering why your life doesn't have the same Instagram filter.

The pitfalls of heavy social media use in relationships are not just about envy-inducing posts. Privacy concerns loom large. Sharing intimate details online can blur boundaries, transforming private matters into public consumption. It's like leaving your diary open in a crowded café—anyone can peek inside. Miscommunication is another lurking danger. In the absence of tone and context, comments can be misinterpreted, leading to misunderstandings that snowball into conflicts. Public interactions on social media can complicate matters further, where a simple like or comment might be misconstrued as something more.

To navigate this digital minefield, it's crucial to establish healthy social media habits that preserve the integrity of your relationships. Setting boundaries for online sharing is a good starting point. Decide what aspects of your relationship should remain offline. Maybe keep that argument about who left the cap off the toothpaste between you two, rather than seeking validation from your followers. Authenticity over curation should be your guiding principle. Share moments that truly reflect your authentic selves, rather than constructing an idealized version of your relationship. This approach fosters genuine connections and diminishes the pressure to maintain a flawless facade.

Yet, let's not throw the digital baby out with the bathwater. Social media can also be a force for good in relationships. For couples separated by distance, it offers a lifeline, keeping the spark alive across time zones. A virtual goodnight kiss or a shared meme can bridge the miles, making absence feel a little less daunting. Furthermore, social media connects you with communities that offer support and advice on relationships, from navigating long-distance love to tackling communication challenges. These virtual support systems can provide comfort and camaraderie when you need it most.

Social Media Balance Guide

1. **Share Intentionally**: Choose moments to share that enhance connection without compromising privacy.
2. **Avoid Comparison**: Remember that everyone's highlight reel isn't the full picture.
3. **Engage Authentically**: Be true to yourself online; authenticity fosters deeper connections.
4. **Limit Screen Time**: Prioritize face-to-face interactions over digital ones whenever possible for richer emotional engagement.
5. **Join Supportive Communities**: Seek out groups that offer genuine support rather than superficial validation.

Balance is key in leveraging social media's potential while safeguarding emotional connections. It's about finding harmony between celebrating life's highlights and preserving its intimate moments, where authenticity reigns supreme over curated perfection. Through thoughtful engagement, you can harness social media's power positively, enhancing connections without losing sight of what truly matters—the people you cherish most.

Case Study: "Read, Seen, Ignored" – Social Media and the Stories We Tell Ourselves

Background:

Jasmine (29, she/her) – An expressive, emotionally attuned woman with *anxious-preoccupied attachment tendencies*.

Liz (31, she/her) – A thoughtful, more reserved partner with *avoidant-dismissive traits*, who prefers privacy and slower emotional pacing.

Version 1: Disconnection Through Assumption and Avoidance

Jasmine had always been active on social media, sharing daily stories, reposting inspirational quotes, and publicly tagging her partner in couple photos. Liz, on the other hand, rarely posted, often muted notifications, and didn't engage much online at all.

One evening, Jasmine posted a photo of the two of them at brunch with the caption: *"Feeling grateful 🤍."* She tagged Liz, expecting her to repost, react, or at least acknowledge it.

Hours passed, and nothing. Jasmine noticed Liz had "seen" the post but hadn't commented or liked it. Instead, she'd posted something unrelated (a landscape photo with no caption).

Jasmine's inner alarm went off. Her nervous system, primed for rejection, began filling in the blanks:

> "Is she embarrassed by me?"

> "Why won't she show she cares publicly?"

> "She reposted her coffee but not me?"

By the time Liz came home, Jasmine was withdrawn and irritable. The eventual confrontation sounded like an accusation:

> "Why do you never show me off? You act like we're not even together online."

Liz, overwhelmed and defensive, pulled back:

> "I don't act like I'm *anything* online. I'm not on there to perform for others. And what does it matter when we are very much together in real life?"

What began as a longing for closeness spiraled into a digital disconnect. Jasmine felt unseen; Liz felt misunderstood. Neither had bad intentions, but both used social media to fill emotional gaps the other hadn't named out loud.

Version 2: Connection Through Clarity and Consent

In therapy, Jasmine and Liz began exploring how social media mirrored their attachment patterns.

Jasmine admitted:

> "When you don't interact with my posts, I feel like I'm reaching and getting silence. It stirs up old stuff—like I'm not chosen."

Liz reflected:

> "I care deeply, but I feel smothered by expectations I didn't agree to. To me, privacy is a way to protect something that's precious."

They agreed on a few shared digital boundaries and practices:

- Jasmine could tag Liz in posts, but with a check-in first if it was intimate or personal.
- Liz agreed to comment or respond in small, consistent ways that felt authentic, like sending Jasmine a DM reaction even if not publicly commenting.
- They created a weekly offline "connection hour" to replace screen-based validation with real-time appreciation.
- Jasmine unfollowed accounts that triggered comparison and instead curated a feed of creativity and shared values.

A few weeks later, Jasmine posted another couple photo, this time with a caption they co-wrote:

"Private in our ways. Public in our joy. Chosen, every day."

Liz responded with a comment and a private message. Jasmine smiled, feeling her affection reciprocated.

They both learned: it's not about the post. It's about the *meaning* we attach to digital silence or engagement, and whether we name that meaning out loud.

Managing Emotional Labor in Modern Relationships

"Invisible work still weighs heavy.
It's time we hold it together, not alone."

Consider emotional labor the unsung hero of relationship dynamics. It's like the backstage crew making the magic happen while the actors take the spotlight. Emotional labor involves managing feelings, smoothing out wrinkles in interactions, and ensuring harmony reigns supreme. It's the glue that holds family and social bonds together, quietly working its magic behind the scenes. Whether it's remembering birthdays, soothing a partner's worries, or playing peacemaker in family feuds, emotional labor keeps relationships ticking along smoothly. Yet, despite its critical role, it often flies under the radar, unrecognized and undervalued.

In every relationship, there is visible labor—dishes, errands, bills—and then there is emotional labor:

- remembering birthdays and important dates
- initiating difficult conversations
- managing the emotional climate in a room
- offering support, anticipating needs, de-escalating tension
- holding space for others while managing your own overwhelm

Emotional labor is the invisible glue that keeps relationships intact. But when it's unspoken or one-sided, it can lead to burnout, resentment, and emotional disconnection.

In many modern relationships, especially where attachment wounds or gender conditioning are at play, one partner often becomes the "emotional manager"—tracking the health of the relationship, initiating repair, maintaining harmony—while the other becomes the "emotional responder." This imbalance isn't always intentional, but it is unsustainable.

Case Glimpse: Nia & Harper

Nia (she/her) and Harper (they/them) had been together for four years. Nia often found herself handling the bulk of emotional tasks: planning date nights, remembering their therapist's advice, checking in when Harper seemed distant, and even managing the dynamics with Harper's family.

Over time, Nia felt exhausted.

> "It's like I'm carrying the weight of 'us' on my own," she admitted. "And Harper doesn't even see it."

Harper, genuinely unaware, responded with defensiveness at first.

> "I didn't know you needed me to do more. I thought everything was fine."

In couples therapy, they began mapping out emotional labor patterns and realized they had never discussed who did what because emotional labor had always been *assumed*, not *assigned*.

Once they saw the patterns clearly, Harper began offering support without being prompted, initiating repair after conflict, even tracking important dates. Nia softened. Their dynamic shifted from quiet resentment to shared responsibility.

Attachment and the Distribution of Emotional Labor

Those with **anxious attachment** may take on *too much* emotional labor, fearing that if they don't hold the relationship together, it will fall apart.

- Those with **avoidant attachment** may unconsciously *evade* emotional tasks, mistaking self-reliance for independence or fearing being seen as "too much.
- **Disorganized attachment** may lead to inconsistency, alternating between over-functioning and emotional withdrawal.
- **Securely attached** partners tend to share emotional labor openly, communicating needs, setting boundaries, and checking in about balance without blame.

When emotional labor is balanced, relationships feel like a team sport, not a solo marathon. When it's imbalanced, even a small disagreement can feel like a collapse. Try to regularly:

1. **Open dialogues about emotional needs and contributions**. By openly expressing what you need emotionally and what you contribute, you create a roadmap for equitable distribution.

2. **Implement systems for checking in regularly**. Think of it as a relationship audit—ensuring tasks and responsibilities are fairly balanced. This might involve setting aside time each week to discuss emotional burdens and redistribute them if necessary.

3. **Encourage gratitude and validation**. Recognition and appreciation of emotional labor can transform this invisible effort into a celebrated contribution. Acknowledge the person who remembers to send flowers on Mother's Day or who listens patiently after a tough day at work. Whether it's through a heartfelt thank-you

note or verbal acknowledgment, recognizing emotional labor fosters a sense of value and respect within relationships

As we navigate these dynamics, it's crucial to remember that emotional labor is not just about keeping peace; it's about maintaining balance. Finding ways to share this load fairly can prevent burnout and nurture healthier connections.

Take a moment to reflect on your own relationship. Who carries the emotional weight? How can you create a more balanced dynamic? Remember, it's not about keeping score but ensuring both partners feel supported and valued in their shared journey.

"Relationships don't thrive because one person carries everything. They thrive when both people feel held, heard, and honored."

When emotional labor is shared with care, not obligation, intimacy deepens. Resentment fades. And love becomes less of a burden and more of a bond.

Activity: The Emotional Labor Ledger

Use this activity to clarify, distribute, and honor the emotional labor in your relationship. It works best when completed together.

Step 1: Identify Emotional Labor Tasks

Start by brainstorming all the tasks that count as emotional labor in your relationship. Here are a few categories to guide you:

Relational Maintenance
- Planning date nights or check-ins
- Initiating tough conversations
- Apologizing or initiating repair

Emotional Support
- Being the "listener" during hard days
- Managing tension in social or family settings
- Anticipating when the other needs space or reassurance

Social & Mental Load
- Remembering birthdays, anniversaries, or gift-giving
- Managing family dynamics or friend conflicts
- Keeping track of appointments, school events, or shared responsibilities

Household Harmony *(even if not physical labor)*
- Tracking when the household feels stressed
- Making suggestions for emotional or logistical balance
- Regulating moods, initiating "us time"

Add your own:

_____

_____

Step 2: Assign (or Reassign) Responsibilities

Next to each task, write:
- if you feel you are currently managing this
- if you *want* to take it on, or enjoy doing it
- if this is something you'd like to redistribute or revisit

Together, agree who will be the primary, shared, or backup person for each task. Focus on strengths, preferences, and capacity—not assumption or tradition.

Step 3: Schedule a Regular Emotional Check-In

Agree on a weekly, biweekly, or monthly check-in. Keep it simple.

Ask each other:
- "Do any of these tasks feel heavier lately?"
- "Have you felt supported emotionally this week?"
- "Is there anything you're holding that I don't see?"

This check-in is not a performance review—it's a chance to stay aligned.

Step 4: Celebrate Contributions

Build in rituals of gratitude for emotional effort. Try:
- A shared note jar where you write down "seen" acts of care
- A monthly toast to each other's growth
- Simply saying, "I noticed when you did that—and it mattered."

Remember: acknowledgment fuels reciprocity. Emotional labor should never feel invisible.

BONUS: Partner Conversation Starter

"I've been thinking about all the invisible things we each do to care for our relationship. Want to sit down together and make sure we're both feeling supported—and seen—for the emotional work we do?"

Ultimately, managing emotional labor is about fostering mutual respect and understanding. By sharing responsibilities fairly and appreciating each other's contributions, you create a nurturing environment where both partners thrive emotionally. So next time you find yourself in the midst of relationship dynamics, remember that balancing emotional labor isn't just about fairness—it's about building connections that withstand life's challenges with grace and empathy.

Cultivating Authenticity in a Fast-Paced World

"In a world that rewards performance, authenticity is a quiet rebellion—and a path to true connection."

Have you ever felt like you're wearing a mask, conforming to what society expects rather than showing your true self? In our rapidly changing world, the pressure to conform can feel overwhelming. Be it the latest fashion trend or the next big tech gadget, the narrative often suggests that fitting in is more important than standing out. But what happens when we constantly mold ourselves to meet these external expectations? We risk losing touch with who we really are. The fear of vulnerability and judgment acts like a heavy anchor, keeping us from surfacing as our authentic selves. It's as if we're walking on eggshells, careful not to reveal too much, lest we face criticism or rejection.

Yet, when we embrace authenticity, a world of relational richness opens up. Imagine connecting with someone on a level so deep that it's like finding a long-lost part of yourself. Authenticity fosters genuine understanding, allowing relationships to flourish in the fertile ground of honesty and trust. It strengthens self-acceptance and confidence, as you're no longer pretending to be someone you're not. The relief of shedding pretense feels like removing tight shoes after a long day—you can finally breathe and move freely.

Why Authenticity Feels Risky in a Fast World

We live in a culture of curation. Email brevity. Social media filters. Workplace small talk. Rapid-fire decisions. It's no wonder so many people default to performative connection: saying what's expected, nodding along, keeping feelings tucked away to "get through the day."

In this speed-driven climate, authenticity can feel like a luxury, or even a threat. But when we habitually choose image over truth, we begin to lose access to our own emotional compass. And over time, this distance between self and expression quietly erodes trust, both in ourselves and in our relationships.

Authenticity is not the same as radical transparency or oversharing. It means being congruent; your outer actions reflect your inner truth.

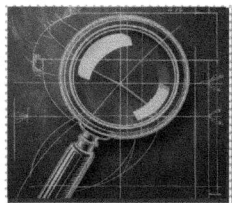

Case Study: Micah in the Conference Room

Micah (41, he/him) is a regional director in a competitive healthcare system. By all external metrics, he's successful—high-performing, articulate, respected by peers. But inside, Micah often feels like a fractured version of himself. He grew up in a household where emotional stoicism was valued. Expressions of need or discomfort were seen as weakness.

In his team meetings, Micah always played the calm, confident leader—even when he felt overwhelmed. He nodded politely at proposals he disagreed with, covered for his burned-out staff, and rarely disclosed when he needed help. He was performing resilience while quietly unraveling.

During a leadership retreat focused on emotionally intelligent communication, a facilitator asked:

"When was the last time you showed up as your full self at work—not the polished version, but the *real* one?"

Micah couldn't answer.

Later that week, he tried something new. At a morning huddle, instead of jumping into updates, he paused:

"Before we dive in—I just want to name that I've been feeling really stretched lately. If anyone else is carrying more than they're letting on, know you're not alone. Let's check in about capacity later today."

The room fell silent. Then slowly, heads nodded. A junior team member messaged Micah afterward:

"Thanks for saying that. I needed to hear it from someone above me."

That one moment of *earned vulnerability* opened a ripple of more honest conversations across the team. Micah didn't become reckless or overly exposed—he became congruent. And his relationships, at work and at home, grew stronger.

Attachment and Authenticity

Those with **anxious attachment** may struggle with authenticity out of fear that honesty will lead to rejection or conflict.

Avoidant-attached individuals may downplay or mask emotional needs, prioritizing control or detachment to feel safe.

Disorganized attachment can cause confusion between impulse and authenticity, acting quickly from fear rather than intentional truth.

Secure attachment fosters an internal sense of worth, making room for both vulnerability and boundaries.

The goal isn't perfect authenticity at every moment. The goal is to practice reconnecting to your truth and choosing self-expression over self-protection, especially when it matters most.

But how do we cultivate authenticity amid the clamor for conformity? One way is through self-reflection and values clarification exercises. By taking time to understand what truly matters to you, you build a foundation that withstands societal pressures. Practicing honesty in your communication is another powerful tool. Speak your truth with kindness and transparency, even when it's uncomfortable. It's like exercising a muscle—the more you do it, the stronger it becomes. These practices create space for authenticity to thrive.

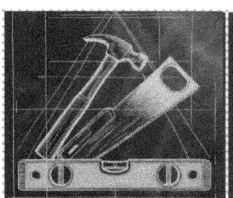

Tool: Practicing Everyday Authenticity

"What might authenticity look like in this moment?"

Use this chart as a practical guide to shift from auto-pilot responses to more authentic choices.

Situation	Default Response (Guarded)	Authentic Response (Aligned)
You're asked how you're doing, but you're stressed	"All good!"	"I'm okay, but it's been a full week. Thanks for asking."
A colleague proposes an idea you have concerns about	Smile & nod	"I see where you're coming from—and I wonder if we might also consider…"

You're emotionally tired but afraid to cancel plans	Push through	"I'd love to connect, but I need to recharge. Can we reschedule?"
A partner or friend misreads your silence	Say "I'm fine"	"I noticed I shut down earlier. I think I was feeling overwhelmed."
You're complimented and feel awkward	Deflect it	"Thank you. That really means a lot."

Tip: Authenticity isn't loud. Often, it's just a truer version of what you were already going to say—spoken with intention instead of instinct.

Authenticity as a Practice, Not a Performance

As we cultivate authenticity in our lives, we're not just enriching our relationships; we're transforming ourselves from within. Authenticity becomes the compass guiding us through life's complexities, ensuring we navigate with integrity and purpose. By embracing who we are, flaws and all, we create space for deeper connections and meaningful experiences.

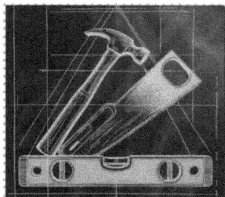

Authenticity Mini-Guides

Mini-Guide 1: Practicing Authenticity in Professional Settings

"Authenticity at work isn't oversharing but aligning your values with your professional style."

Small Shifts Toward Authenticity:
- Replace "I'm fine" with:
    → "I'm managing a lot this week—appreciate you checking in."
- When disagreeing:
    → "I hear where you're coming from. I'd like to add another perspective."
- In a moment of overwhelm:
    → "Can we revisit this after I regroup? I want to give it the attention it deserves."
- When needing clarification:
    → "I'm not sure I fully understand—could you walk me through that again?"

Boundaried Vulnerability Looks Like:

Naming emotions without spilling them:
    → "I care about this outcome, and I'm feeling some pressure around it."
- Advocating for yourself without over-explaining:
    → "I don't have capacity for that right now, but I can revisit it [date/time]."

Authentic Professional Values May Sound Like:
- "I value direct communication, even when it's uncomfortable."
- "I want to contribute in ways that feel honest, not just expected."
- "I appreciate workplaces where humanity is part of the process."

Mini-Guide 2: Practicing Authenticity in Friendships

"Authenticity in friendship means showing up as who you are—not who you think they want you to be."

Small Shifts Toward Authenticity:
- When you're not okay:
    → "I don't have the energy to hang out, but I'd love to reconnect soon."
- When something stings:
    → "Hey, I know you didn't mean anything by it, but that comment stuck with me."
- When you need more from the friendship:
    → "I really value you—and I've been missing deeper check-ins. Can we carve out some space for that?"

Boundaried Vulnerability Looks Like:
- Naming your needs *and* your care:
    → "I don't expect you to fix this—I just need a friend to sit with it for a minute."
- Saying no with clarity, not guilt:
    → "I want to support you, and I also need to take care of myself right now."

Authentic Friendship Values May Sound Like:
- "We don't keep score, but we keep each other close."
- "We can say hard things kindly."
- "We don't need to be available all the time to still be committed."

Mini-Guide 3: Practicing Authenticity in Romantic Partnerships

"Intimacy deepens through truth shared gently and consistently."

Small Shifts Toward Authenticity:
- Instead of withdrawing:
    → "I'm feeling a little tender right now. Can I have a few minutes and then talk?"
- Instead of appeasing:
    → "I want to say yes, but I need to check in with myself first."
- Instead of assuming:
    → "I'm wondering if we're okay—I'm noticing a shift in energy."

Boundaried Vulnerability Looks Like:
- Sharing your truth without blame:
    → "When you went quiet last night, I felt distant from you. I want to understand what was going on."
- Owning your own reactions:
    → "I noticed I got defensive. That's mine to work through—and I want to stay in the conversation."

Authentic Relationship Values May Sound Like:
- "We name what we feel, even when it's messy."
- "We ask for reassurance, not proof."
- "We repair—not just resolve—when we hurt each other."

In closing this chapter on navigating modern relationship challenges, remember that authenticity is a continuous journey of self-discovery and acceptance. It's about choosing to show up as your true self in a world that often demands conformity. As you cultivate this authenticity within yourself, you'll find that it reverberates through your relationships, enriching them with depth and understanding.

Authenticity takes courage because it invites uncertainty. But it also invites *real* connection. And with each moment you honor your internal truth, especially when it feels vulnerable, you send a message to your nervous system:

"It's safe to be me here."

That message, repeated, becomes a foundation. A relationship. A new norm.

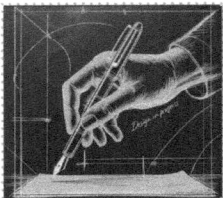

Authentic Moment Tracker

"Small, honest choices build the bridge between who we are and how we relate."

Use this tracker to become more aware of your everyday opportunities for authenticity. Practice noticing moments where you had a choice and reflect on what shaped that choice.

Step 1: Identify Your Authenticity Opportunities (Daily or Weekly)

Complete the following prompts as they arise, or during a reflective practice at the end of the day/week:

1. A moment today where I acted out of habit or self-protection instead of truth:
2. What I said or did in that moment:
3. What I *really* felt or needed beneath that response:
4. What I wish I had said or done instead (if anything):
5. What made it hard to respond authentically? (Fear, people-pleasing, time pressure, etc.):
6. What might help me choose authenticity next time in a similar moment?

Step 2: Celebrate Authentic Wins

Don't just track misalignments—honor the moments you *did* show up truthfully, even in small ways.

1. A moment I chose authenticity today:
2. How it felt in the moment:
3. How the other person responded (if relevant):
4. What I learned about myself from that moment:

Step 3: Pattern Awareness (Optional Weekly Review)

At the end of each week, use these prompts to track themes:

- Where in my life is authenticity most natural for me?
- Where do I still feel the need to perform, manage impressions, or shrink my truth?
- What beliefs might be driving that dynamic?
- One small, aligned action I can take this week to be more congruent is:

Partner/Colleague Prompt (Optional)

"I'm working on showing up more honestly and gently, even in small ways—would you be open to checking in about that with me sometime?"

Holistic Well-being and Relationship Building

There's a kind of exhaustion that doesn't just settle into your bones—it seeps into your identity.

That was the phase of our relationship after becoming parents. The survival years. The everything-is-urgent years. My body had barely healed, our baby needed constant care, and work didn't stop for either of us. In the face of these demanding priorities—my son, my spouse, our home, our schedules—my own wellness felt like a luxury I couldn't afford.

But of course, that's when it matters most.

When you feel like you have nothing left for yourself... that's the moment you must return to yourself.

I began clawing my way back. Slowly. Quietly. Imperfectly. Small acts of wellness—stretching for five minutes, breathing before speaking, journaling after everyone was asleep. I had to rebuild trust in my own body and emotions. I had to re-learn how to hear myself in a house full of other voices.

Paul was doing the same.

It was his first true self-love journey. For a man conditioned to prioritize structure, responsibility, and performance, this wasn't a natural shift, but it was a necessary one. He began setting boundaries, listening to what gave him energy and what drained it. He started naming his needs. Not perfectly, but more often. He stopped seeing rest as weakness. He stopped seeing joy as optional.

One brutal battle he faced was with his job.

It was a significant source of tension in his life and, by extension, in our home. He was consistently frustrated, disappointed, and disillusioned by his work. And even when he tried not to bring it home, it followed him. In his tone. In his energy. In his distance. Everything felt colored by his discontent.

I encouraged him more times than I can count to find something new. But for Paul, a man raised to sacrifice and equate provision with love, it wasn't that simple. Leaving a steady job felt like abandoning duty. Risking our stability felt selfish.

Then something shifted.

After a year or more of practicing consistent, holistic self-care like movement, mindfulness, creative expression, and therapy, he finally began to feel the value of his own happiness. He began to understand that joy wasn't a bonus, but a form of presence. And presence was what the people who loved him needed most.

He finally leaped and left the job.

And the man who came home to us afterward was not the same one from every morning before.

His courage changed something in me as well.

It inspired me to fight for my own joy again. To permit myself to pursue something that had lived quietly inside me for years—writing. A dream I'd carried since I was eight years old, scribbling stories in notebooks. A voice I'd hushed in the name of responsibility and finally chose to amplify in the name of becoming.

Because when we take care of ourselves as a daily act of devotion instead of an afterthought, we show up for others in ways we never imagined. We love more deeply. We give more freely. We start to believe in the goodness we can bring into the world again.

And we never really know how our healing will ripple outward.

But it's almost always more beautiful than we expected.

WELL-BEING ISN'T A SIDE QUEST; it's the foundation of how we show up in every relationship we care about. When we feel nourished, we listen differently. When our nervous systems are calm, we connect more easily. When we treat ourselves with compassion, we model that same compassion for the people we love.

In the next chapter, we'll explore the essential link between personal wellness and relational health. You'll learn how your emotional, physical, mental, and spiritual well-being all shape the way you attach, express, and connect. You'll be invited to build relational habits that heal—not just for you, but for the people walking beside you.

Because the healthiest relationships don't ask us to choose between love and selfhood.

They're built by people brave enough to choose both.

The Interconnected Self: How Personal Wellness Shapes Connection

"How we care for ourselves quietly teaches others how we want to be loved."

Your emotional patterns, thought habits, energy levels, and internal sense of worth shape your relationships. Whether you're loving from a grounded place or from burnout, whether you're reacting from fear or responding with clarity, your inner state sets the tone for how you connect.

This is the essence of interconnected wellness: we don't relate in isolation—we relate through the state of our nervous systems, minds, and internal stories.[36]

When you tend to your well-being, your relationships benefit:

- You communicate more clearly
- You co-regulate more effectively
- You repair with less shame
- You honor boundaries without guilt

You don't need to be "fully healed" to love well, but attending to your emotional hygiene, physical balance, and internal clarity makes love feel safer, not more complicated.

Four Dimensions of Personal Wellness that Shape Relational Health

1. **Emotional Wellness**

Recognizing your emotions, understanding their origins, and expressing them honestly are foundational for secure connection.

Suppressed feelings often emerge in sideways behaviors (e.g., sarcasm, blame, withdrawal) that erode intimacy.[63]

> Try: Pause and name what you're feeling. "I'm feeling overwhelmed and tender right now. I need a moment to regroup."

2. **Physical Wellness**

Your body is the first interpreter of safety. A dysregulated nervous system will read a neutral silence as rejection or a delayed response as abandonment. Sleep, nourishment, hydration, and rest aren't luxuries; they're relationship tools.[65]

> Try: When activated, place your hand on your chest and say, "Right now, I'm safe. I can respond from calm."

3. **Mental Wellness**

Your beliefs about yourself and others become the lens through which you hear tone, interpret nonverbal cues, or predict outcomes. Unchecked, these scripts distort intimacy. With mindfulness and mental rest, you can begin responding to your partner as they are, not as your fear imagines.

> Ask: "Is this thought coming from truth or from habit?"

4. **Spiritual Wellness**

Spiritual wellness doesn't require religion. It's about connection to something larger than the self, such as meaning, values, purpose, or wonder.

When your spiritual needs are unmet, relationships can take on too much weight—becoming your sole source of worth or identity. When spiritual wellness is nurtured, you are more rooted in something enduring. We come to relationships with more curiosity, presence, and perspective.

Try: Reflect weekly on the question, "What values are guiding how I show up in love this week?"

Your well-being isn't separate from your relational health. It *is* your relational health. The more attuned you are to your inner world, the more spacious, safe, and sustainable your connection with others becomes.

> *"We bring all of us into love—our minds, our bodies, our histories, our hopes. And we get to shape how those parts meet each other and show up in the world."*

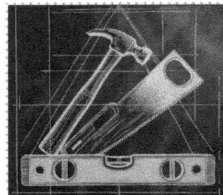

Holistic Relationship Wellness Inventory

"Before I ask what's happening between us, I ask what's happening within me."

This tool can be completed individually or together with a partner. Its purpose is to spark insight and to offer direction for deeper alignment.

Step 1: Self-Reflection Across the Four Domains

Rate each area on a scale of 1–5:
1 = rarely true; 3 = sometimes true; 5 = consistently true.

Emotional Wellness
- I can name my emotions as they arise
- I know how to self-soothe when I feel dysregulated
- I express how I feel without blaming or withdrawing
- I can receive my partner's emotions without feeling overwhelmed
- I reflect on my reactions instead of acting on impulse

Subtotal (out of 25):

Physical Wellness
- I sleep regularly and wake up feeling somewhat rested
- I move my body in ways that support my energy
- I eat in a way that stabilizes my mood
- I notice when my body is stressed and take action
- I bring physical presence (touch, presence, attention) into my relationships

Subtotal (out of 25):

Mental Wellness
- I'm aware of my internal self-talk
- I can notice when I'm catastrophizing, ruminating, or assuming
- I reflect before reacting in conversations
- I set mental boundaries around time, input, or overthinking
- I stay curious about my interpretations in conflict

Subtotal (out of 25):

Spiritual Wellness
- I feel connected to something greater than myself
- I engage in regular practices that bring me meaning (meditation, nature, service, creativity)
- I live according to values I've defined, not just inherited
- I bring those values into my relationships
- I feel purpose in how I love and relate

Subtotal (out of 25):

Step 2: Review Your Totals

You may notice:
- Higher scores in one area = stability and strength to draw from
- Lower scores = a gentle signal to bring more attention, not shame

Total Score (out of 100):
- Which domain feels most nourishing to you right now?
- Which domain feels most depleted or overlooked?

Step 3: Aligning with Intention

Choose one area you'd like to focus on this month. Then answer:
1. I want to feel more _____ in this area of wellness because...
2. One small daily or weekly action I can take is...
3. How I hope this will impact my relationships is...

Optional Partner Check-In

Use this prompt with your partner or a close friend:

"What's one area of wellness you're working on within yourself—and how can I support that growth in a way that feels good for you?"

Body, Mind, Bond: A Resilience Framework for Modern Relationships

Resilient love is forged by how we self-regulate in hard moments, how we interpret each other's behavior, and how we repair after disconnection. The Body-Mind-Bond model offers a three-part framework for strengthening emotional resilience in relationships, working from the inside out.

1. **Body: The Nervous System's Role in Relational Safety**

Before we speak, before we choose a response, our body reacts. That reaction is shaped by past attachment wounds and life experiences. It is not a sign of some character flaw, but a survival response.

Signs of dysregulation include:
- Emotional flooding
- Withdrawal or shutdown
- Escalated defensiveness
- Somatic anxiety (tight chest, heat, freeze)

Learning to recognize and regulate your nervous system helps de-escalate conflict and promote repair.[66]

Practice: Grounding through breath before responding in moments of stress. "I'm noticing my chest tightening. I'll take a few breaths before we continue."

2. **Mind: Emotional Hygiene and Internal Dialogue**

Resilience requires tending to our internal narratives. Are you assuming the worst, spiraling in silence, or reacting from scripts written long ago?

Without emotional hygiene, we:
- Interpret silence as rejection
- React to tone as criticism
- View love through a lens of past pain

With regular reflection, therapy, or journaling, we begin to unhook from these patterns and relate more intentionally.

Ask: "Is my reaction about this moment—or something older?"

3. **Bond: Relational Habits That Build Safety Over Time**

A clear mind and calm body help, but your daily behaviors are what solidify trust. Emotional resilience in love comes from small, consistent practices that say: *I am here, even when it's hard.*

Resilient bonds are built through:
- Repair after conflict
- Rituals of reconnection (check-ins, shared routines)
- Emotional bids and attuned responses
- Validation without fixing

Try: A daily micro-ritual—"One thing I appreciated about you today..."—to strengthen connection even in hard weeks.

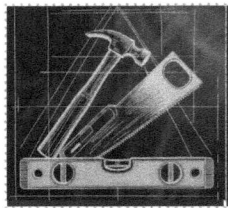

Relational Check-In: The BMB Inventory

Try this brief self-check weekly:

Area	Questions	Notes
Body	Have I been sleeping, moving, or breathing in ways that regulate me?	
Mind	Have I been holding helpful or harmful stories about myself or my partner?	
Bond	Have we shared moments of closeness, repair, or intention this week?	

Even a few minutes of reflection can shift you from reactivity to reconnection.

In Practice: The Interplay

- When your **body** is grounded, your **mind** interprets more clearly.
- When your **mind** is centered, your **bond** feels safer.
- When your **bond** feels secure, your **body** and **mind** relax.

This feedback loop is the heart of relational resilience.

"Resilient love is not built in perfect days. It's built in the tiny moments where we stay, soften, breathe, repair, and try again."

You don't need to master everything at once. Begin with one: body, mind, or bond.

Each step you take toward your own wellness strengthens the bridge between you and the ones you love.

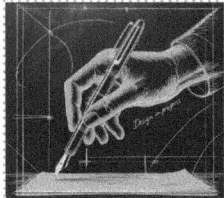

Mind Maintenance Tracker

"Tend to your thoughts like you tend to a garden—pull the weeds, water the roots, and rewrite what no longer fits."

Instructions

Use this tracker once a day (or 2–3x per week) to check in with your inner dialogue, identify harmful or outdated scripts, and practice reframing with compassion. You may choose to journal on it, discuss it with a partner, or keep it private as part of your emotional hygiene routine.

Daily / Weekly Mind Check-In

Prompt	Today's Insight
1. What emotion did I carry today that lingered beneath the surface?	
2. What story did I tell myself about that emotion or situation?	

3. Is that story helpful, hurtful, or inherited?

4. What would I say to a friend who was thinking that same thing?

5. What's a more supportive, believable version of that story I can try on? *(revised script)*

6. Did I speak to myself kindly today? If not, when did the tone shift?

7. What can I remind myself tomorrow that supports self-trust and clarity?

Optional Add-Ons for Deeper Integration

Daily Anchor Phrase:

Write one simple affirmation or reframe to carry with you into tomorrow.

Today's Anchor Phrase:

"_____"

Quick Mood Recap

Circle or write the emotions that showed up most for you today:

| Calm | Confused | Frustrated | Sad | Grateful | Anxious | Loved | Numb |

Other words that describe my state today:

Reflection Prompt (weekly)

"One script I'm ready to stop rehearsing is..."

_____

"One belief I'm beginning to trust more fully is..."

_____

Closing Thought

This tracker is about returning to your truth more often than your fear and letting your mind become a space that reflects the compassion, clarity, and curiosity you offer others.

Wellness Isn't Solo Work: Building Relational Habits that Heal

> *"Some healing only happens in safe connection. We were hurt in relationship—and we can be healed in one, too."*

The Myth of Independent Healing

Modern self-help culture often glorifies the image of the lone, self-actualized individual: meditating in silence, journaling by candlelight, retreating inward to fix all wounds alone. While solitude has value, healing isn't a closed-door endeavor. In truth, much of our pain was shaped in relationships, and it's often through relationships that we learn how to feel safe, seen, and whole again.

This is the heart of relational wellness: healing not *from* people, but with people. Not because others rescue us, but because they co-create the conditions for nervous system safety, emotional regulation, and secure attachment to flourish.

Co-Regulation: Your Nervous System in Relationship

At the core of relational healing is co-regulation—the ability to calm or stabilize your nervous system through safe, responsive connection.

Co-regulation happens in micro-moments:

- A calm hand on your back during overwhelm
- Eye contact that softens your breath
- A partner saying "I'm here" while you're spiraling
- The tone of voice that says *"You're safe with me"*

For those with attachment wounds, especially those who were ignored, invalidated, or emotionally neglected, co-regulation can be reparative. It teaches your nervous system a new story:

"I don't have to carry this alone."

Co-regulation is not dependency. It's not "you fix me." It's a practice of shared emotional presence that allows both partners to return to center together.

Mutual Care: A Two-Way Flow of Nourishment

In healthy relationships, wellness is reciprocal. It's not one person holding emotional labor while the other coasts. It's not tit-for-tat. Instead, it's an attunement to each other's needs, capacity, and cycles.

Mutual care might look like:

- Checking in: "Do you have space to listen right now, or should we revisit this later?"
- Offering care without being asked: "You seem drained—can I take something off your plate?"

- Making room for each other's growth: "I want to support this new chapter of yours. What does that look like?"
- Naming your own limits without guilt: "I love you, and I need time to refill myself before I can really be present."

Mutual care doesn't always mean doing the same thing. It means valuing each other's well-being as *shared*. We are still independent beings in our attachments, but not isolated.

Shared Rituals: The Anchor in the Everyday

Rituals are not just routines. They are intentional habits of connection—acts that say, "We matter, and we're making space to return to each other."

These rituals don't need to be grand. Often, the simplest ones hold the most meaning:

- A 10-minute "morning check-in" over coffee
- Friday evening walk-and-talks
- Tech-free dinners once a week
- A monthly reflection ritual: *"What helped us feel connected this month? What got in the way?"*

Shared rituals offer predictability in a chaotic world, especially important for those with insecure attachment or trauma histories. They create relational muscle memory; reminders that love can be steady, not just reactive.

Shared Rituals Builder Worksheet

"The little things we do with intention become the strong things we stand on together."

Step 1: Reflect Individually

Take a moment to consider what helps *you* feel safe, seen, and emotionally close in a relationship.

Prompts:
1. What do I tend to crave most in connection?
2. *(e.g., time together, laughter, deep talks, physical touch, spiritual alignment)*
3. What small moments make me feel emotionally anchored or "home" in this relationship?
4. When I look back on times we felt most connected, what were we doing consistently?
5. What types of rituals feel nourishing—not obligatory—to me?

Step 2: Explore Together

Set aside intentional time (20–30 minutes) to share your reflections and co-create connection rituals that feel supportive for both of you. Aim for **sustainable over elaborate**.

Daily Rituals

Choose one small action you can commit to doing *most* days.

Examples:
- Morning 5-minute eye-contact + intention setting
- Bedtime "one thing I appreciated about you today"
- A shared check-in phrase (e.g., "How's your heart?")

Ours:

Weekly Rituals

Choose one consistent space for check-in, closeness, or play each week.

Examples:
- Sunday "state of us" walk or coffee
- Screen-free evening together
- A gratitude or affirmation ritual

Ours:

Monthly or Seasonal Rituals

Choose something slightly more involved or reflective that you return to periodically.

Examples:
- A shared journaling ritual
- A creative or spiritual practice (vision board, tarot pull, playlist swap)
- A check-in on personal and relationship goals

Ours:

Repair & Reconnection Ritual

Discuss how you'd like to reconnect after disconnection or conflict. Ritualizing this can reduce fear and increase repair readiness.

Examples:
- A mutual "pause + return" phrase
- Writing notes after conflict to share and reflect
- A pre-agreed soft re-entry ritual (e.g., silent hug before talking)

Ours:

Step 3: Celebrate Your Rituals

Choose how you'll acknowledge and protect your rituals:

How will we track our rituals without pressure?

What will we do when we drift from them
(as all couples sometimes do)?

How will we celebrate a month of consistency or reconnect after falling off?

Final Commitment

"We choose to build rituals that nourish—not drain—our connection. Our time together is not just shared—it is sacred."

Signed (Optional):

Partner A:

Partner B:

Date:

Relational Wellness Supports Individual Growth

"Healing isn't a solo climb. It's a shared rhythm—where one heartbeat steadies another, and each small act of presence becomes a building block for trust."

A common fear, especially in avoidant or hyper-independent individuals, is that relationships will get in the way of personal development. But when built with intention, relational habits can become the scaffolding that helps you grow even more fully.

A healing relationship will never require you to shrink to fit it. Instead, it says:

"You don't have to become smaller to be close. And you don't have to walk alone to be whole."

When wellness is practiced together:

- Self-care becomes shared care
- Boundaries are honored, not feared
- Growth is not an exit from intimacy—it's a reason to deepen it

We are not meant to regulate, repair, or rise entirely on our own. Relational wellness doesn't mean losing yourself in another. It means building something that makes both of you more whole in the process, and in the presence of each other.

Practicing Self-Compassion: A Path to Deeper Connections

> *"The way you speak to yourself becomes the emotional climate you offer others."*

Self-Compassion As a Relational Foundation

Many people believe that connection begins with giving more—more attention, more energy, more love. But the truth is, relationships are not nourished by depletion. They are nourished by wholeness, and wholeness begins with how we treat ourselves.

Self-compassion is the courageous practice of treating yourself with the same tenderness, understanding, and grace you would offer someone you love. And it changes how you show up in your relationships. It is not self-pity or avoiding accountability, because it is a practice grounded in love. It is a practice that seeks to liberate our full potential.

When we practice self-compassion, we:

- Reduce reactivity and shame spirals during conflict
- Increase our capacity to offer empathy without resentment
- Set boundaries from worthiness, not fear
- Repair more quickly—both with others and with ourselves

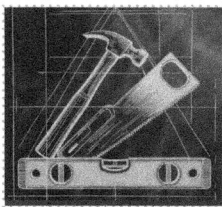

3 Pillars of Self-Compassion (Kristin Neff's Model)

1. **Mindfulness**—Naming what's happening without exaggerating or suppressing
2. → "This is hard."
3. **Common Humanity**—Remembering you are not alone in your struggle
4. → "Others have felt this too."
5. **Self-Kindness**—Speaking to yourself with warmth instead of harshness
6. → "I'm allowed to hurt and still deserve care."

Practiced together, these create *inner safety*—the foundation for outer connection.

Your self-compassion creates space for empathy to emerge instead of defensiveness. When we are constantly attacking ourselves instead of offering an internal safe harbor, we are already primed to protect and defend. While this instinct isn't inherently bad, it can build a counterproductive habit of defensiveness during connection opportunities.

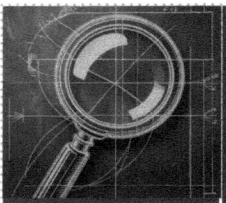

Case Glimpse: Leo & Emotional Rewiring

Leo (35, he/him) had always prided himself on being a good partner. He showed up with consistency, shared household tasks, and cared deeply for his long-term partner, Camille. But whenever conflict arose, Leo's inner world turned volatile. Raised in a home where emotional expression was either punished or pathologized, he'd internalized the belief that *messing up meant being unlovable*.

After arguments, Leo didn't just feel regret—he felt worthless. His inner critic would roar:

> *"You're a screw-up."*

> *"She's going to leave."*

> *"You're emotionally broken."*

Camille, meanwhile, felt shut out. She experienced Leo's spiral not as remorse, but as disconnection.

> "It's like when things get hard, he disappears into himself. I want repair, not self-punishment."

In therapy, Leo began learning the language of self-compassion. One session shifted everything when the therapist gently said:

> *"You're not taking accountability when you collapse into shame—you're abandoning yourself. And when you do that, you can't be present to repair with Camille."*

Leo had never thought of it that way. He had believed that berating himself was *being responsible*. But he slowly came to see that shame wasn't the same as accountability—it was a wall that blocked intimacy. He started practicing a new internal script:

> "This was a painful moment, not a defining one. I didn't show up how I wanted to—but I care enough to stay in it."

The next time he and Camille argued—over a forgotten anniversary plan—he felt the familiar tug of shame begin to rise. But instead of withdrawing, he paused, grounded his breath, and said:

> "I can see how this landed hard. It makes sense you're hurt. I want you to know I didn't mean to dismiss the day—but I understand that's how it felt."

Camille softened. Leo stayed present. He didn't lead with defense. He didn't spiral into self-blame. He owned his impact, acknowledged his intent, and showed up with self-compassion and care.

Later, Leo reflected:

> "I always thought that admitting I was wrong would confirm I was unlovable. Now I see that admitting I messed up, *without turning on myself*, actually makes me more available—for repair, for intimacy, for connection."

For the first time, Camille felt like they were on the same team during conflict, not opponents. And Leo began to experience what it felt like to be in a relationship where accountability didn't require self-erasure.

By speaking kindly to himself, Leo opened a new emotional doorway with his partner.

When we consistently exercise self-compassion, we remove the reason to raise an internal shield. Instead, we remain open to what our loved one might be trying to express. We can hear their words instead of drowning them out with our own internal reprimands. From there, empathy—or the willingness to put ourselves in another's shoes—is much easier.

"When I soften toward myself, I stop needing others to rescue, fix, or define me. I become safer to connect with—because I am safe within myself."

Attachment & Self-Compassion

Your attachment style often shapes your inner voice:

- **Anxious attachment** tends to carry inner criticism: "I'm too much," "I ruined it again."

- **Avoidant attachment** often minimizes self-needs: "I shouldn't feel this," "I don't need anyone."

- **Disorganized attachment** can experience chaotic or conflicting self-talk: "I'm broken," "I have to protect myself, but I wish I didn't have to."

Self-compassion interrupts these patterns. It teaches your nervous system: *"I can make mistakes and still be worthy. I can have needs and still be loved."*

Judging Intention or Impact

Self-compassion is not about justifying or excusing all of your behavior. It's about creating enough internal safety to examine what happened without collapsing into self-condemnation. Instead of fusing your identity with your mistakes (*"I am the problem"*), self-compassion invites a more nuanced truth: *"I made a choice that didn't align with who I want to be, and I can take responsibility while still being worthy of care."*

This includes recognizing the difference between intention and impact: you can acknowledge that your actions caused harm, even if you didn't mean to, and still meet yourself with honesty rather than harshness. In doing so, self-compassion becomes a path to true accountability. Because when you are not busy defending your worth, you are free to own your impact, learn, and grow. In this way, self-compassion is not a shield from change but the foundation for sustainable, self-led improvement.

In arguments with loved ones, this kind of self-compassion can be transformational. When tensions rise, it's easy to slip into defensiveness: *"I didn't mean to hurt you, so why are you upset?"* or *"I messed up again—I'm just impossible to love."* But with self-compassion, you learn to hold both truths: your intentions may have been innocent, *and* your impact may have been painful. Instead of spiraling into shame or deflecting blame, you can say, *"I see that what I did hurt you. That wasn't my intent, but I take responsibility for how it landed."* This response not only deepens emotional maturity but also builds relational trust. Because when you can stay kind to yourself in the face of imperfection, you're more available to stay kind to others, too.

Just as we can be harsh with ourselves when we fall short, we're often just as quick to judge others by their impact while ignoring their intention. In conflict, it's common to leap to conclusions—*"They don't care," "They're selfish," "They always do this"*—because their behavior hurts us. But when we're operating without compassion, we forget that others, too, are navigating their own histories, triggers, and blind spots.

Self-compassion helps us extend grace outward: if we can believe that *we* are still worthy even when we mess up, we become more able to hold that same possibility for others. This doesn't mean tolerating harmful behavior or abandoning boundaries—it means staying curious, not punitive. It's the emotional maturity to ask, *"Could this be a mistake rather than malice?"* and to recognize that most people, like us, are imperfect humans trying—sometimes clumsily—to love and be loved.

Self-Compassion in Relationships Sounds Like...
- "I didn't show up how I wanted to—and I still love myself enough to try again."
- "I'm having a hard time, and I don't need to pretend I'm fine."
- "It's okay to need space. It doesn't make me cold or broken."
- "I'm learning how to care for me *and* stay close to you."

Self-compassion is not just a personal practice, but also a relational offering.

Because when you stop abandoning yourself, you create the kind of presence that others feel safe to come home to.

Reflection Prompts for Practicing Self-Compassion

Choose one to explore in writing or aloud with someone you trust:

- "What's something I judged myself for recently—and what would I say to a friend in the same situation?"
- "What's a mistake I keep replaying—and what truth have I forgotten about myself?"
- "What belief about worthiness am I ready to gently question?"
- "Where can I practice softness today, without waiting for someone else to give me permission?"

08

Sustaining Growth and Transformation

So, where did all of that leave Paul and me?

Not in some picture-perfect ending, but in something far more real: a love that continues to unfold—steadier, deeper, and more rooted in choice than ever before. We are wholly independent. Gratefully attached. Still growing.

I couldn't have imagined the years and experiences that would follow that quiet afternoon.

What began as a vulnerable exchange turned into a thousand conversations, tiny shifts, new rituals, and a new phase of our relationship. A phase where we were no longer held hostage by the neuro-behavioral patterns formed from our earliest attachments. A phase where we got to choose love. Choose our better selves. Choose each other—for a connection richer and more fulfilling than either of us had known was possible.

Today, our story continues, but with more compassion, more resilience, and more trust in our capacity to repair, recalibrate, and return to each other.

We don't try to be everything for one another anymore. That, we've learned, is one of the most liberating signs of secure love. We both have friendships that anchor us, people we can turn to for clarity and care when we feel untethered. People who remind us who we are and how far we've come. And we offer the same in return.

When I'm feeling off-balance, one of my dearest friends gently asks,

"What do you know to be true?"

It's a question that brings me back every time.

Because the truth is, I can't predict what lies ahead—not in our marriage, not in our lives, not in a world that changes by the minute. But I do know who we are becoming. I know how we practice love. I know the rhythms we've cultivated, the support we've welcomed, the openness we've protected. I know how we show up.

And that means I no longer fear attachment, nor do I cling to it.

I experience it—with presence, with gratitude, with wonder.

Because I trust myself now.

Because I trust us.

Because that's what I know to be true.

… And maybe that's the real definition of "happily ever after."

Creating Lasting Change: Habits for Secure Attachments

> *"Secure attachment isn't a trait you're born with—it's a pattern you practice, over and over again."*

As you now know, your attachment style is not fixed. It is not a sentence—it's a strategy your nervous system developed to keep you safe. And strategies can evolve. With awareness, intention, and repeated relational experiences, you can rewire toward **earned security**—a felt sense of safety, consistency, and trust in yourself and others.

But insight alone doesn't create change. Lasting transformation happens through small, practiced habits that align with secure functioning over time.

Secure attachment is something we *do*, not something we *have*.

 The Habits that Strengthen Secure Attachment

Here are five foundational practices that, over time, create a secure inner and relational foundation:

1. Emotional Check-Ins

"What am I feeling right now—and what do I need?"

Secure individuals tune into their emotional state and name it, without shame or suppression. This creates a baseline for self-attunement, which is necessary before you can fully attune to others.

Practice:

At least once a day, pause to name your emotional state and one need. Even 30 seconds of self-honesty builds your emotional fluency over time.

2. Communicating Needs Clearly

> *"I'm not needy; I need closeness because I'm human."*

Secure attachment includes the confidence to ask for what you need without apology. It also means being able to hear someone else's needs without taking it personally.

Practice:

Use "I feel... I need..." statements in both low-stakes and emotionally charged moments. (Example: "I'm feeling overwhelmed and could really use some reassurance.")

3. Repairing Instead of Reacting

> *"When conflict happens, I don't leave. I lean in, and work to make it safe again."*

Conflict is inevitable. What defines secure functioning is the ability to own impact, return to regulation, and engage in genuine repair.

Practice:

After a disagreement, ask yourself: *"What was my part in this?"* and *"What would a healing step look like?"* Then take it, even if it's small.

4. Regulating Without Withdrawing

> *"When I'm dysregulated, I slow down to not shut down."*

Insecure attachment often leads to overwhelm or shutdown during stress. Secure individuals recognize their window of tolerance and pause for regulation without abandoning the relationship.

Practice:

Learn your body's cues for overwhelm. Use co-regulation tools (breath, grounding, music, connection) and name your process: *"I need a few minutes to calm down so I can respond clearly."*

5. Offering Reassurance & Relational Consistency

> *"I want you to know I'm here and I'm not going anywhere just because we hit a bump."*

Secure attachment is built through repeated moments of reliability, not grand gestures. A quick check-in, a kind word, a follow-through—these are the invisible threads that make love feel safe.

Practice:

Create micro-rituals of safety:

- A daily "thinking of you" text
- A shared phrase after conflict (e.g., "Still us.")
- A weekly check-in where each person answers: *"What helped me feel close to you this week?"*

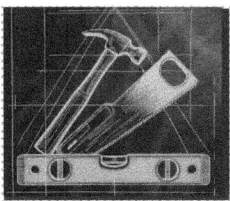

Secure Habits Weekly Tracker

> *"Attachment security is built through daily intention more than grand moments."*

How to Use This Tracker

Each day, reflect on whether you engaged in the following secure attachment practices. Mark each box with a **C**, **P**, or **M** to symbolize **c**ompletion, **p**artial effort, or **m**indful awareness—even if you didn't follow through.

At the end of the week, reflect gently: Which habits felt natural? Which stretched you? What supported your consistency?

Weekly Tracking Table

Day	1. Emotional Check-In	2. Clear Need Expression	3. Repair or Accountability	4. Regulation Without Withdrawal	5. Reassurance or Relational Ritual
Mon					
Tue					
Wed					
Thu					
Fri					
Sat					
Sun					

End-of-Week Reflection Prompts

1. Which secure habit felt most natural or energizing to me this week? Why?
2. Which habit felt most challenging or unfamiliar? What got in the way?
3. What small support, reminder, or ritual could make that habit easier next week?
4. One moment I felt proud of how I showed up in a relationship was…

Gentle Reminder

"Healing isn't about never slipping into old patterns—it's about noticing sooner, responding kinder, and trying again without shame."

Reflective Journaling For Ongoing Insights

Reflective journaling is one of the most accessible and powerful tools for generating ongoing insight. By putting thoughts, emotions, and experiences into words, we begin to see patterns, name needs, and recognize moments of growth we might otherwise overlook. Unlike reactive thinking, journaling slows the mind and allows us to observe ourselves with curiosity rather than judgment. Writing serves to clarify emotional patterns, illuminating behaviors and reactions you might not consciously recognize. This clarity isn't just enlightening; it empowers decision-making and enhances problem-solving skills in profound ways. By observing these patterns, you become adept at predicting your emotional responses and guiding them toward healthier manifestations.

As you continue this practice, notice how it evolves. Let each page be a testament to your journey—a living document reflecting not just where you've been, but where you're heading with purpose and clarity. Embrace this tool with humor on challenging days and gratitude on enlightening ones, knowing that every word you write is a significant step closer to the person you aspire to be.

Change Feels Small—Until It's Real

Many people expect attachment healing to feel dramatic or sudden. But real growth often feels quiet. It's reaching out instead of retreating. It's staying in the room a few seconds longer. It's pausing before reacting. It's saying what you mean and meaning what you say.

Over time, these small acts become your new normal. All because you've practiced trusting yourself.

> *"Security isn't something we demand from others. It's something we co-create through the choices we repeat."*

You don't have to transform overnight.
You just have to begin—then begin again.

Engaging with a Support Network: Building a Community

"Secure relationships don't just happen between two people. They're sustained within a web of care."

We're Wired for Belonging

Human beings are biologically designed to thrive in connection, not isolation. For thousands of years, our survival depended on the village, the extended family, and the neighbor who noticed. In today's world, the "village" often feels like it's vanished, replaced by digital feeds, busy schedules, and a quiet epidemic of loneliness.

But healing attachment wounds and sustaining secure relationships require more than just inner work or one romantic bond. They ask us to rebuild the village. To create intentional, reciprocal support systems that help us feel safe, known, and nourished.

Community is a form of emotional infrastructure: the scaffolding that holds us steady when one connection falters or we're growing in new directions.

Why a Support Network Matters for Attachment Health

"We don't heal by becoming more independent. We heal by becoming safely interdependent."

Attachment injuries often involve unmet needs for reliability, attunement, or repair. Those injuries rarely heal in a vacuum. A supportive network offers:

- **Co-regulation**: friends or loved ones who help calm and stabilize us when we're emotionally activated
- **Perspective**: trusted others who offer clarity when we're stuck in old narratives or relational patterns
- **Resource-sharing**: emotional, practical, and sometimes even logistical support during stressful life phases
- **Proof of safety**: multiple experiences of being seen, heard, and valued help reinforce secure internal beliefs

Building a Support Network with Intention

"I don't have to rely on one person to be everything. I can build a circle of care that holds me in different ways."

Creating meaningful community in adulthood can feel daunting. Thankfully, we don't have to strive for quantity, but rather quality, consistency, and shared emotional availability.

Here's how to start cultivating your circle of support:

1. **Assess Existing Connections**
   Reflect:

   - Who in my life consistently sees and hears me?
   - Where do I feel emotionally safe enough to be imperfect?
   - Who do I feel nourished by, not drained?

   Start by noticing the relational gold already present and consider how to nurture those bonds more intentionally.

2. **Name and Invite In**
   Secure attachment includes the ability to express need without shame. This might sound like:

- "I've been trying to be more intentional about staying connected. Would you want to connect monthly?"
- "When I talk to you, I feel grounded. I'd love to make more space for this friendship."
- "I'm working on asking for help more—can I run something by you sometime?"

These small invitations can open new dimensions of connection.

3. **Diversify the Emotional Portfolio**
   One person can't meet every need. Consider:

   - A friend who's great at humor and lightness
   - A mentor who offers grounding and wisdom
   - A peer navigating similar emotional or relational terrain
   - A therapist, group, or healing space for deeper exploration

Think of this as your relational nervous system: different parts supporting different functions.

4. **Offer What You Hope to Receive**
   Community is built through reciprocal vulnerability and generosity. Show up how you'd like others to show up for you.

   - Send the check-in text first
   - Share your appreciation, even if it feels small
   - Make space for others to need you, too

Your relationships don't have to be perfect to be secure. A secure community is built through mutual care, repairing missteps, and consistency over time. When you surround yourself with people who meet you with presence, honesty, and warmth, you reinforce the most important truth of all:

"I am not alone. I am held. I am part of something bigger than my wounds."

Case Glimpse: Mina & the Circle She Built

Mina (28, she/her) had always been the "strong one." In friendships, she was the listener, the planner, the helper. But after a painful break-up, she realized she had few people who knew how to hold *her* in her messiness.

In therapy, Mina unpacked a belief she had carried since childhood:

> "If I ask for support, I'll become a burden."

She began experimenting with vulnerability in small doses. She texted an old friend and asked to talk through something heavy, resisting the urge to stop after a cheerful update. The friend responded warmly. Mina cried, but from relief instead of sadness.

Over the next year, she created intentional rhythms with a handful of trusted people: a biweekly walk with a friend, a Sunday call with her cousin, and a healing circle she joined online.

> "It's not just that I have people," Mina said. "It's that I finally let them have *me*."

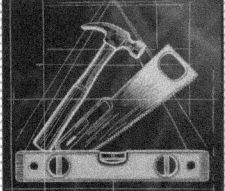

Practical Ways to Create or Expand Your Community

Building a support network in adulthood often requires intentionality, vulnerability, and patience—especially if you've been conditioned to rely solely on yourself or hesitate to trust others. Below are realistic, attachment-informed ways to grow your circle of connection without overwhelming your nervous system or forcing inauthentic relationships.

1. Start Small—and Start With One

You don't need a dozen new friends. Start by strengthening one connection:

- Reconnect with someone you drifted from
- Reach out to a friend who feels safe but undernourished
- Invite someone you admire for a low-pressure conversation (walk, coffee, voice note exchange)

Try this script:

"I've been craving more real connection lately—would you be open to catching up sometime soon?"

2. Join Spaces Where Emotional Presence Is the Norm

Look for communities where intentional connection is already woven in:

- Support or process groups (grief, parenting, anxiety, identity-based)
- Book clubs or creative circles with reflective check-ins
- Movement or wellness classes that include mind-body awareness
- Online healing communities, if in-person feels overwhelming

Choose a setting where people are already *showing up with their inner lives*, not just their resumes.

3. Build Reciprocity Through Rhythm

Consistency builds safety. Propose a repeating ritual:

- A weekly text check-in
- A monthly dinner rotation
- A shared Google calendar for mutual support goals
- A voice memo thread to stay connected across time zones

Relational depth doesn't always come from more time—sometimes it comes from regular time.

4. Practice "Low-Stakes Vulnerability"

You don't have to bare your soul to feel connected. Instead, try:
- Sharing one honest feeling in conversation ("This week's been a lot for me emotionally.")
- Offering a personal insight or small struggle
- Asking a thoughtful question that invites depth ("What's something that's been quietly hard for you lately?")

When you model softness, you signal safety.

5. Release the Fantasy of Effortless Community

It's easy to assume "real" community should come naturally—but many people are also lonely, waiting, and unsure how to reach out.

It's not needy to initiate. It's brave. And it's how networks begin.

"Community isn't found. It's built through the courage to be seen and the willingness to stay."

BONUS: Partner Conversation Starter

Bonus Prompt: Starting the Conversation

If you're unsure how to start building a deeper connection, try saying:

"I've been thinking about how important it is to have people you can grow with—not just talk to. I'd love to be more intentional about supporting each other if that ever feels right to you."

Celebrating Progress: Acknowledging Your Journey

Acknowledging progress is an affirmation that reinforces your motivation and commitment, making the work less daunting and more rewarding. When you take the time to notice how far you've come, it's like adding logs to the fire of your determination, stoking it to continue burning bright even when the gusty winds of life threaten to snuff it out.

So make sure to weave joy into the journey, appreciating the lessons learned along the way, and using those insights as fuel for further transformation. Whether it's through pages of thoughtful journaling, gatherings with cherished friends, or quiet, introspective moments of reflection, make space for recognition in the rhythm of your life. As you continue this ever-evolving path of emotional growth, know and remind yourself that each step forward is worth heralding, each milestone a testament to your resilience and commitment to becoming the best version of yourself.

Each time you celebrate progress, you strengthen the foundation of the community you're building because you begin to trust that connection can be earned, sustained, and real. The work of creating a support network isn't just about finding the right people. It's about becoming someone who can receive care as much as offer it, someone who shows up not because they've healed everything, but because they're willing to grow alongside others. Remember: meaningful community isn't built overnight. It's built through consistent presence, mutual repair, and the courage to be just a little more seen than you were yesterday. Keep showing up. You are not behind—you are becoming. And there are people out there waiting to build something beautiful with you.

The Future of Attachment: Adapting to New Challenges

> *"Attachment is not a fixed system but a living framework, capable of growing with us."*

Attachment Is Evolving—and So Are We

When John Bowlby first introduced attachment theory in the mid-20th century, he rooted it in the biological imperative for infants to form secure bonds with caregivers to survive. Over time, researchers like Mary Ainsworth, and later, Sue Johnson and others, helped expand the model into adult relationships—revealing how our early experiences shape how we connect, protect, and repair throughout life.

But the world Bowlby described looks very different today.

We're navigating global stressors, digital intimacy, identity shifts, and cultural redefinitions of family and partnership. As our relational contexts evolve, so too must our understanding of attachment. It must function as a fluid, adaptable framework we can carry into the future with intention and care.

Emerging Insights in Attachment Theory

Recent research and therapeutic perspectives are expanding what we know about attachment:

- **Attachment style is contextual, not fixed.** You might be securely attached in friendships but avoidant in romantic relationships or anxious in high-stress environments. This nuance is helping people move away from rigid labels and toward relational flexibility.

- **Attachment isn't just interpersonal—it's also systemic.** Social trauma, racialized attachment wounds, and marginalization impact how safe people feel to bond, express need, or seek support. Culturally attuned attachment models are now emerging to account for these realities.

- **Earned security is more attainable than previously believed.** Research shows that consistent, emotionally available relationships, even later in life, can help rewire insecure patterns and create a felt sense of safety.

- **Attachment styles can interact in dynamic, non-binary ways.** Many people experience blended or shifting styles over time. There is growing emphasis on attachment behaviors and capacity for repair over static style labels.

- **Digital intimacy is reshaping how we attach.** We now form and maintain relationships through screens, voice notes, and texts. While these can offer accessibility and connection, they also introduce challenges in reading emotional cues and regulating in real time.

Adapting to What's Ahead: Relational Resilience in a Changing World

While change is inevitable, secure attachment remains a steady compass. The future of connection doesn't ask us to be perfect, but asks us to become more curious, self-aware, and collaborative in how we relate.

Here are a few key ways to adapt:

1. **Stay Fluid, Not Fixed**
   "My attachment patterns describe where I've been. They don't determine where I'm going."

Let your attachment identity remain flexible. You are allowed to evolve. Avoid over-identifying with labels and instead focus on building behaviors that align with secure functioning.

Try this: Replace *"I'm anxious"* with *"I notice I seek reassurance quickly when I feel uncertain—and I'm learning to regulate that."*

2. **Prioritize Repair Over Perfection**

In an increasingly fast-paced and fractured world, misunderstandings are inevitable. What matters most is your willingness to circle back, own impact, and reconnect.

Try this: When things go sideways, ask: *"What would repair look like here, not just resolution?"*

3. **Bring Mindfulness to Digital Attachments**

The digital world will only grow more entangled with our relationships. Practice conscious digital intimacy. Engage with intention, clarify tone, and don't substitute online gestures for embodied presence.

Try this: Ask loved ones, *"What helps you feel connected online, and what makes you feel distant?"*

4. **Self-Regulate to Co-Regulate**

As external stressors fluctuate, the ability to self-regulate becomes essential. Inner stability creates outer availability.

Try this: Build a "nervous system menu" of tools that help you ground, reset, and re-open—breathwork, movement, music, self-talk, sensory input.

5. **Bear Witness, Be Witnessed**

Future-proof attachment by sharing your growth process with the people in your life. Let them witness your shifts and embrace invitations into theirs.

Try this:
- "I'm learning how to stay when things get uncomfortable. Thanks for your patience."
- "I'm working on asking for what I need instead of waiting to be rescued."

The Future Is Secure—If We Choose It

"Attachment is not who you are; it's what you practice."

The future of attachment will be shaped by how we choose to show up:

- With gentle accountability instead of blame
- With curiosity over certainty
- With presence over perfection

As the world shifts, so will relationships. But the core truth remains: a secure connection is still possible. Not because the world slows down, but because you've slowed down enough inside yourself to respond with clarity, care, and courage.

The future of attachment isn't about holding on to what was. It's about co-creating what comes next—with heart, with healing, and with hope.

Notes:

CONCLUSION

Returning to Yourself, Reaching for Connection

What you've held in your hands is more than a workbook. It's a blueprint for becoming—rooted in the science of attachment, the art of relationship, and the sacred, often messy practice of emotional growth. If you've made it this far, you've likely discovered what many never do: healing doesn't mean fixing yourself. It means remembering who you are beneath the defenses you had to build to survive.

Throughout these pages, we've explored how attachment patterns are shaped, how they can be rewired, and how they show up in our relationships with partners, children, families, friends, and communities. We've confronted emotional hijacks and quiet fears, celebrated the power of repair, and practiced the language of empathy, self-compassion, and accountability. Together, we've charted a course from inherited patterns to intentional partnership—from survival strategies to relational security.

And perhaps most importantly, we've reminded ourselves that change doesn't happen in the abstract. It happens in micro-moments:

- A breath before reacting
- A hand offered during conflict
- A truth spoken gently instead of swallowed
- A habit of connection practiced again and again

Your nervous system can learn new rhythms. Your relationships can become safe places to land. You can live—and love—from a place of earned security, even if you didn't start there.

There is no perfect version of you waiting at the end of this book. There is only *this version*—a version more aware, more open, and more deeply connected than before.

And that, Reader, is enough. That is the work. That is the way home.

Author's Note

Dear Reader,

Thank you for walking this path with me.

Whether you read every word or picked up what you needed, I hope this book reminded you of something essential: you are not broken, and you are not alone. You are a human being wired for connection, healing, and growth—and you are capable of transforming the way you love and are loved.

I didn't write this book from the mountaintop of mastery. I wrote it from the middle of the work—from the tender, complicated, beautiful space where real change happens. And I wrote it for people like you: people willing to examine their patterns, tell the truth, and take small steps toward a more connected life.

If this book helped you show up even 1% more honestly, kindly, or courageously in your relationships, then it has done its work.

Keep practicing. Keep returning. Keep becoming.

You are already the author of your next chapter.
And I'm cheering for you, every step of the way.

With gratitude and hope,
Helen Harper

References

1. Bowlby J. *Attachment and Loss: Volume I. Attachment*. New York, NY: Basic Books; 1969.

2. Ainsworth MDS, Blehar MC, Waters E, Wall S. *Patterns of Attachment: A Psychological Study of the Strange Situation*. Hillsdale, NJ: Lawrence Erlbaum; 1978.

3. Mikulincer M, Shaver PR. *Attachment in Adulthood: Structure, Dynamics, and Change*. 2nd ed. New York, NY: Guilford Press; 2016.

4. Cassidy J, Shaver PR, eds. *Handbook of Attachment: Theory, Research, and Clinical Applications*. 3rd ed. New York, NY: Guilford Press; 2016.

5. Klohnen EC, Bera S. Behavioral and experiential patterns of avoidantly and securely attached women across adulthood: A 31-year longitudinal perspective. *J Pers Soc Psychol*. 1998;74(1):211–223.

6. Lamb ME. Nontraditional families and childhood development. Child Dev. 2012;83(3):1046–1049.

7. Siegel DJ, Hartzell M. Parenting from the Inside Out: How a Deeper Self-Understanding Can Help You Raise Children Who Thrive. New York, NY: TarcherPerigee; 2013.

8. Farr RH, Patterson CJ. Coparenting among lesbian, gay, and heterosexual couples: Associations with adopted children's outcomes. Child Dev. 2013;84(4):1226–1240.

9. van den Dries L, Juffer F, van IJzendoorn MH, Bakermans-Kranenburg MJ. Fostering security? A meta-analysis of attachment in adopted children. Child Youth Serv Rev. 2009;31(3):410–421.

10. Cyr C, Euser EM, Bakermans-Kranenburg MJ, van IJzendoorn MH. Attachment security and disorganization in maltreating and high-risk families: A series of meta-analyses. Dev Psychopathol. 2010;22(1):87–108.

11. Howes C. Social-emotional classroom climate in child care, child-teacher relationships and children's second grade peer relations. Soc Dev. 2000;9(2):191–204.

12. van IJzendoorn MH. Intergenerational transmission of parenting: A review of studies in nonclinical populations. Dev Rev. 1992;12(1):76–99.

13. Main M, Kaplan N, Cassidy J. Security in infancy, childhood, and adulthood: A move to the level of representation. Monogr Soc Res Child Dev. 1985;50(1–2):66–104.

14. Slade A, Grienenberger J, Bernbach E, Levy D, Locker A. Maternal reflective functioning, attachment, and the transmission gap: A preliminary study. Attach Hum Dev. 2005;7(3):283–298.

15. Siegel DJ. The Developing Mind: How Relationships and the Brain Interact to Shape Who We Are. 3rd ed. New York, NY: Guilford Press; 2020.

16. Fonagy P, Steele M, Steele H, Moran GS, Higgitt AC. The capacity for understanding mental states: The reflective self in parent and child and its significance for security of attachment. Infant Ment Health J. 1991;12(3):201–218.

17. Schore AN. Effects of a secure attachment relationship on right brain development, affect regulation, and infant mental health. Infant Ment Health J. 2001;22(1–2):7–66.

18. Rothbaum F, Weisz JR, Pott M, Miyake K, Morelli G. Attachment and culture: security in the United States and Japan. Am Psychol. 2000;55(10):1093-1104.

19. Keller H. Cultural models, socialization goals, and parenting ethnotheories: A multicultural analysis. J Appl Dev Psychol. 2003;24(6):613-616.

20. Miyake K, Morelli G. Cultural aspects of infant attachment: Japanese and U.S. children in the Strange Situation. In: Rothbaum F, ed. Attachment Theory and Close Relationships. New York, NY: Guilford Press; 2000.

21. Mesman J, van IJzendoorn MH, Sagi-Schwartz A. Cross-cultural patterns of attachment: Universal and contextual dimensions. In: Cassidy J, Shaver PR, eds. Handbook of Attachment: Theory, Research, and Clinical Applications. 3rd ed. New York, NY: Guilford Press; 2016:852–877.

22. Grossmann KE, Grossmann K, Spangler G, Suess G, Unzner L. Maternal sensitivity and newborns' orientation responses as related to quality of attachment in northern Germany. In: Parkes CM, Stevenson-Hinde J, Marris P, eds. Attachment Across the Life Cycle. London, UK: Routledge; 1991.

23. Keller H. Universality claim of attachment theory: Children's socioemotional development across cultures. PNAS. 2018;115(45):11414–11419.

24. Parke RD, Gauvain M. Child Psychology: A Contemporary Viewpoint. 8th ed. New York, NY: McGraw-Hill Education; 2013.

25. Elder GH. Children of the Great Depression: Social change in life experience. Westview Press; 1999.

26. Arnett JJ. Emerging adulthood: A theory of development from the late teens through the twenties. Am Psychol. 2000;55(5):469–480.

27. Twenge JM. Generation Me: Why Today's Young Americans Are More Confident, Assertive, Entitled—and More Miserable Than Ever Before. New York, NY: Atria Books; 2014.

28. Barry CT, Sidoti CL, Briggs SM, Reiter SR, Lindsey RA. Adolescent social media use and mental health from adolescent and parent perspectives. J Adolesc. 2017;61:1–11.

29. Bartholomew K, Horowitz LM. Attachment styles among young adults: A test of a four-category model. J Pers Soc Psychol. 1991;61(2):226–244.

30. Fraley RC, Waller NG, Brennan KA. An item response theory analysis of self-report measures of adult attachment. J Pers Soc Psychol. 2000;78(2):350–365.

31. Goleman D. Emotional Intelligence: Why It Can Matter More Than IQ. New York, NY: Bantam Books; 1995.

32. Salovey P, Mayer JD. Emotional intelligence. Imagin Cogn Pers. 1990;9(3):185–211.

33. Kabat-Zinn J. Wherever You Go, There You Are: Mindfulness Meditation in Everyday Life. New York, NY: Hyperion; 1994.

34. Chiesa A, Serretti A. Mindfulness-based stress reduction for stress management in healthy people: A review and meta-analysis. J Altern Complement Med. 2009;15(5):593–600.

35. Tang YY, Hölzel BK, Posner MI. The neuroscience of mindfulness meditation. Nat Rev Neurosci. 2015;16(4):213–225.

36. Siegel DJ. The Mindful Brain: Reflection and Attunement in the Cultivation of Well-Being. New York, NY: W. W. Norton & Company; 2007.

37. Neff KD. Self-compassion: An alternative conceptualization of a healthy attitude toward oneself. Self Identity. 2003;2(2):85–101.

38. Siegel DJ. Mindsight: The New Science of Personal Transformation. New York, NY: Bantam Books; 2010.

39. Bradshaw J. Homecoming: Reclaiming and Championing Your Inner Child. New York, NY: Bantam Books; 1990.

40. Pollak S. Self-Compassion for Parents: Nurture Your Child by Caring for Yourself. New York, NY: Guilford Press; 2019.

41. Siegel DJ, Bryson TP. The Whole-Brain Child: 12 Revolutionary Strategies to Nurture Your Child's Developing Mind. New York, NY: Delacorte Press; 2011.

42. Southwick SM, Charney DS. Resilience: The Science of Mastering Life's Greatest Challenges. 2nd ed. New York, NY: Cambridge University Press; 2018.

43. Tugade MM, Fredrickson BL. Resilient individuals use positive emotions to bounce back from negative emotional experiences. J Pers Soc Psychol. 2004;86(2):320-333.

44. Lieberman MD, Inagaki TK, Tabibnia G, Crockett MJ. Subjective responses to emotional stimuli during labeling, reappraisal, and distraction. Emotion. 2011;11(3):468-480.

45. Neff KD. Self-compassion, self-esteem, and well-being. Soc Personal Psychol Compass. 2011;5(1):1-12.

46. Bonanno GA. Loss, trauma, and human resilience. Am Psychol. 2004;59(1):20-28.

47. Brown B. Daring Greatly: How the Courage to Be Vulnerable Transforms the Way We Live, Love, Parent, and Lead. New York, NY: Gotham Books; 2012.

48. Gilbert P, Irons C. Focused therapies and compassionate mind training for shame and self-attacking. In: Gilbert P, ed. Compassion: Conceptualisations, Research and Use in Psychotherapy. London, UK: Routledge; 2005:263-325.

49. Neff KD. Self-compassion and psychological well-being. In: Baumeister RF, ed. Encyclopedia of Social Psychology. Thousand Oaks, CA: SAGE Publications; 2007:735-737.

50. Gottman JM, Silver N. The Seven Principles for Making Marriage Work. New York, NY: Harmony Books; 2015.

51. Johnson SM. Hold Me Tight: Seven Conversations for a Lifetime of Love. New York, NY: Little, Brown Spark; 2008.

52. Cordova JV, Gee CB, Warren LZ. Emotional skillfulness in marriage: Intimacy as a mediator of the relationship between emotional skillfulness and marital satisfaction. J Soc Clin Psychol. 2005;24(2):218–235.

53. Rosenberg MB. Nonviolent Communication: A Language of Life. Encinitas, CA: PuddleDancer Press; 2003.

54. Linehan MM. Skills Training Manual for Treating Borderline Personality Disorder. New York, NY: Guilford Press; 1993.

55. van der Kolk B. The Body Keeps the Score: Brain, Mind, and Body in the Healing of Trauma. New York, NY: Viking; 2014.

56. Levine A, Heller R. Attached: The New Science of Adult Attachment and How It Can Help You Find—and Keep—Love. New York, NY: TarcherPerigee; 2010.

57. Tatkin S. Wired for Love: How Understanding Your Partner's Brain and Attachment Style Can Help You Defuse Conflict and Build a Secure Relationship. Oakland, CA: New Harbinger; 2012.

58. Prager KJ, Roberts LJ. Deep intimate connection: Self and intimacy in couple relationships. In: Mashek DJ, Aron A, eds. Handbook of Closeness and Intimacy. Mahwah, NJ: Lawrence Erlbaum Associates; 2004:43–61.

59. Chapman G. The 5 Love Languages: The Secret to Love That Lasts. Chicago, IL: Northfield Publishing; 1992.

60. Chapman G, White P. The 5 Love Languages: Singles Edition. Chicago, IL: Northfield Publishing; 2004.

61. Egbert N, Polk D. Speaking the language of relational maintenance: A validity test of Chapman's five love languages. Communic Res Rep. 2006;23(1):19–26.

62. Gottman JM. Why Marriages Succeed or Fail: And How You Can Make Yours Last. New York, NY: Simon & Schuster; 1994.

63. Linehan MM. DBT Skills Training Manual. 2nd ed. New York, NY: Guilford Press; 2015.

64. Gottman JM, Declaire J. Raising an Emotionally Intelligent Child. New York, NY: Simon & Schuster; 1997.

65. Shanker S. Self-Reg: How to Help Your Child (and You) Break the Stress Cycle and Successfully Engage with Life. New York, NY: Penguin; 2016.

66. Porges SW. The Pocket Guide to the Polyvagal Theory: The Transformative Power of Feeling Safe. New York, NY: W. W. Norton & Company; 2017.

67. Thompson RA. Emotion regulation: A theme in search of definition. Monographs of the Society for Research in Child Development. 1994;59(2–3):25–52.

68. Perry BD, Szalavitz M. The Boy Who Was Raised as a Dog: And Other Stories from a Child Psychiatrist's Notebook. New York, NY: Basic Books; 2006.

69. Center on the Developing Child at Harvard University. Building the Core Capabilities for Life: The Science Behind the Skills Adults Need to Succeed in Parenting and in the Workplace. 2016.

70. Fivush R. The development of autobiographical memory. *Annu Rev Psychol.* 2011;62:559–582.

71. Cozolino L. *The Neuroscience of Human Relationships: Attachment and the Developing Social Brain.* 2nd ed. New York, NY: Norton; 2014.

72. Twenge JM, Campbell WK. *The Narcissism Epidemic: Living in the Age of Entitlement.* New York, NY: Atria; 2009.

73. Hughes D, Baylin J. *Brain-Based Parenting: The Neuroscience of Caregiving for Healthy Attachment.* New York, NY: Norton; 2012.

74. Ungar M. Change Your World: The Science of Resilience and the True Path to Success. Toronto, Canada: Sutherland House; 2019.

75. Siegel DJ, Bryson TP. The Power of Showing Up. New York, NY: Ballantine Books; 2020.

76. Gopnik A. The Gardener and the Carpenter: What the New Science of Child Development Tells Us About the Relationship Between Parents and Children. New York, NY: Farrar, Straus and Giroux; 2016.

77. Levine PA. Waking the Tiger: Healing Trauma. Berkeley, CA: North Atlantic Books; 1997.

78. Schwartz RC. No Bad Parts: Healing Trauma and Restoring Wholeness with the Internal Family Systems Model. Boulder, CO: Sounds True; 2021.

79. SAMHSA. Trauma-Informed Care in Behavioral Health Services. Treatment Improvement Protocol (TIP) Series 57. Rockville, MD: Substance Abuse and Mental Health Services Administration; 2014.

80. Fallot RD, Harris M. Creating Cultures of Trauma-Informed Care (CCTIC). Community Connections; 2009.

81. Herman JL. Trauma and Recovery. New York, NY: Basic Books; 1992.

82. Rothschild B. The Body Remembers: The Psychophysiology of Trauma and Trauma Treatment. New York, NY: Norton; 2000.

83. Main M, Solomon J. Discovery of an insecure-disorganized/disoriented attachment pattern. In: Brazelton TB, Yogman MW, eds. Affective Development in Infancy. Norwood, NJ: Ablex; 1986:95–124.

84. Hughes DA. Building the Bonds of Attachment: Awakening Love in Deeply Troubled Children. 2nd ed. Lanham, MD: Rowman & Littlefield; 2006.

85. Neff KD. Self-Compassion: The Proven Power of Being Kind to Yourself. New York, NY: William Morrow; 2011.

86. Ford JD, Courtois CA. Treating Complex Traumatic Stress Disorders: An Evidence-Based Guide. New York, NY: Guilford Press; 2009.

www.ingramcontent.com/pod-product-compliance
Lightning Source LLC
Chambersburg PA
CBHW040003040426
42337CB00033B/5209